Common Market Suicide

Common Market Suicide

by

A.K. Chesterton

The A.K. Chesterton Trust

2017

Printed and published in 2017.

© **The A.K. Chesterton Trust, BM Candour, London, WC1N 3XX, United Kingdom.**

Website: www.candour.org.uk

This enlarged and expanded second edition is:

ISBN: 978-0-9932885-9-3 (Paperback)

ISBN: 978-1-912258-02-4 (Hardback)

The first edition of this book was first published in 1977.

This booklet is dedicated to our founder and patriot, A.K. Chesterton.

"Never shall we allow it to be said that in the hour of treason there were no Britons to keep faith with the past or hand down a torch to the future."

Candour # 520, March 1972.

A.K. Chesterton, 1899 -1973.

SOUNDING THE REVEILLE DEPENDS ON US

Specially drawn for Candour by John Jackson

Contents

Foreword to the second edition.. Page 11

I. High Treason ....Page 15

II. Champagne or the Rocks...Page 20

III. Hell-Bent for the Dark.. Page 27

IV. U.S. Bulldozing Britain into Europe............................ Page 38

V. This Fateful Year.. Page 49

VI. Britain's Blackest Hour.. Page 54

VII. Open Letter to Edward Heath....................................... Page 60

VIII. Hold High the Torch .... Page 65

IX. Appeal to The Queen... Page 70

X. Stand Fast!... Page 79

XI. We Must Get Out... Page 83

XII. Confound their Politics.. Page 90

XIII. Europe - The Truth.. Page 95

Appendix 1. The Treaty of Rome.. .... Page 106

Foreword to the second edition

This second edition of *Common Market Suicide* was originally going to contain the same text as the 1977 first edition, but upon reading A.K. Chesterton's other brilliant anti-E.E.C. *Candour* leading articles between 1971 and 1973, the decision was taken to expand it considerably by including them. They were too powerful to be allowed to languish in the aging pages of back-issues of *Candour* any longer.

The first edition was put together by Rosine de Bounevialle four years after the death of A.K. Chesterton when the British cause was at a low ebb, and all seemed lost. Britain was committed to the Common Market - as most Britons then considered it - despite A.K's desperate attempts to warn the British public that this was merely a stage on the way to a federal Europe and world government.

"...may all find the spirit, the steadfastness and the self-sacrifice to fight for the recapture of our country—a country delivered into the hands of usurers by their political agents, who have at last forced us into the Augean stables of Europe. Candour was the first journal in the United Kingdom to give battle against the Marketeers, and this battle we have sustained for the better part of twenty years. The task would have been impossible but for the support of our loyal readership and we would not ask for that support to be continued, and indeed reinforced, were we not convinced that the battle can still be won. We owe it to those who come after us never to accept defeat."

The decades passed, and resistance to the European Union grew, slowly at first, but by 2015 David Cameron's Conservative Party were forced to grant the British people an in/out referendum as part of their 2015 General Election manifesto. This was forced by internal party pressures as well as by the 'leave' cause, headed by Nigel Farage. Whatever we think of Mr Farage, there would not have been a referendum without his efforts.

The Conservatives then won the 2015 general election to everyone's surprise, and had to make good on their referendum pledge, one that they felt sure would be an easy win for 'remain'. The 'remain' camp was backed by all the major political parties, the entire establishment, most of the media, every 'expert' under the sun, foreign governments and politicians, celebrities and even the Archbishop of Canterbury.

I have to confess that I went to bed on the evening of the referendum of 23rd June 2016 believing that the 'remain' camp would win easily, and our only - and last - chance of restoring Britain as a sovereign nation was about to be extinguished forever.

Awakening the next morning, I was profoundly shocked to hear that the British people had - at last - ignored the easy option and had risen against the establishment system. They had voted to leave the European Union.

A year later, the negotiations have only just begun, but the Conservative party (the same party which took us in!) have - on the surface anyway - backed the 'Brexit' decision, and are engaged in what look set to be bitter negotiations with the implacable EU. Theresa May's rash and foolish gamble to increase her parliamentary mandate backfired in June 2017, and it now is beginning to appear that some Conservatives are preparing to backslide on a full exit from the EU.

We will no doubt have to fight the treacherous 'remain' camp all the way, and we must keep in mind that our bid for freedom is a victory secured by the British **people** against tremendous odds. The rest of Europe - and indeed the world - is watching our bid to free ourselves. This has been a profound blow to the 'world government' process, and has shown that that the British and the nation state will not lie down and face extinction quite yet.

Whatever happens in the months ahead, the British people have sent a clear signal to Parliament that we are unhappy in being ruled by the EU, and we cannot possibly go on with the integration forced upon us.

We must constantly re-iterate that we do not hate the races and nations of Europe, only the monolithic evil that is the European Union. A nation state can trade with other states. It does not have to submit to being ruled by our so-called trading partners.

I would like to thank Jeff Carson for proof reading the text and James Mitchell for his help with the cover design.

In closing, I hope that A.K. Chesterton and Rosine de Bounevialle are resting more easily now that a national renaissance is apparently underway.

Rob Black

The A.K. Chesterton Trust
August 2017

I

HIGH TREASON

By A. K. CHESTERTON

Candour # 511, June 1971.

THERE was a time, and this not long ago, when a conspiracy to commit high treason — which still carries the death penalty in Britain — used secret signs and pass-words, took shape in underground cellars and pursued its nefarious aims deeply hidden from the public gaze: it was an evil emanation of the night. Today, what a difference!

Today not only does treason walk the street in the full light of day, not only does it proclaim its purpose from the house-tops — it commands the air, dominates the newspapers, usurps the pulpits and has as its chief declared protagonist the British Government, whose leader does not hesitate to risk his immortal soul by telling an outrageous lie in furtherance of its objective.

I refer to the most damnable plot to surrender the historic national independence of Great Britain to a cabal set up by the European Economic Community, not answerable to any elected body and most palpably the brain-child of the Lords of International Finance. The lie which I ascribe to the Right Honourable (sic) Edward Heath[1] is his almost unbelievable assurances to the House of Commons that Britain's membership of the E.E.C. does not entail "an erosion of essential national sovereignty."

---

[1] **Sir Edward Richard George Heath**, (1916 – 2005), was a British politician who, as Prime Minister 1970 -1974, took the country into the then European Economic Community.

* * * *

This preposterous statement, loudly cheered by the mindless Tory back-benchers, was not challenged by the Opposition, which preferred to mark-time and talk about the need to secure the right terms for entry. The parrot-cry of "right terms" has been used by both Conservatives and Labour for the last decade to suggest that the terms have still to be negotiated, whereas in truth they were laid down years ago — in the Treaty of Rome[2].

If Members of Parliaments are not aware of the provisions of that Treaty, then they are irresponsible ignoramuses not fit to be entrusted with the affairs of a Parish Council, while for those who are aware of them some harsher description must be found. The only one which seems to me adequate is that they are conscious traitors.

They must know that immediately Great Britain signs the Treaty of Rome she relinquishes all power to manage her own economic affairs and must allow the goods of her European partners to enter the country duty free while those from her faithful daughter nations overseas are obliged to jump a tariff wall. Nobody is better aware of this fact than Edward Heath, who in his speech at Harvard in March 1967, said that "a new range of subjects which are the essence of politics, for example the form of taxation or the level of social security, will have to be added to those taken by the Community as a whole," which — as the Anti-Common Market League rightly points out — means that "in plain English, all important economic decisions will be made in Brussels, not Westminster." Nor, as Heath also knows, will it be the making of economic decisions alone which are taken out of our hands. Every enactment of the bureaucratic cabal in Brussels will immediately have the force of law in Britain and this covers pretty well the entire range of public affairs. Bureaucrats, being paid, will not be the real masters empowered to order our lives.

---

[2] See Appendix 1.

Their masters will be the Overlords of Monopoly Capitalism, who have long been planning the overthrow of the nation state.

A sidelight on the situation is perhaps to be glimpsed in two utterances by Harold Lever, M.P., the leader of the Labour Party's pro-Common Market task force. Mr. Lever last month went on record proclaiming that Britain's membership of the Common Market was "essential not only for her future prosperity, and no less for her safety." His second statement was quoted in the May *Candour* and read: "The basic solution (of the currency problem) lies in the creation of a world reserve bank which would create an internationally-accepted reserve unit to replace both dollars and sterling." For those who have minds to comprehend, these two statements taken in conjunction make clear the direction of the international policy drive. Not that Lever himself necessarily knows anything about that!

* * * *

However, it is worth taking a look at the "safety" aspects of the E.E.C. Western Germany has had to cope with a fantastically large number of senior service officers suborned to spy for the Russians. So, to only a slightly less extent, has Italy. France is not unfamiliar with the problem. We have had our "Blakes," our "Lonsdales," our "Fuchs" and various other "guests." Is it not certain that the European Community, with its larger milieu, would be a Devil-inspired Tom Tiddler's ground for espionage agents and saboteurs of every sort and condition? Would treason not permeate every nook and cranny? Is it conceivable that after three or four years we would be left with a single military or technological secret to call our own?

Furthermore, were the manufacture of our arms components to be distributed in accordance with internationalist planning, with parts of our fighters or bombers or missiles being made in Germany, France, Italy, Belgium or elsewhere on the Continent, what a rich harvest would be gathered in by the first tidal wave of a Soviet advance!

There would be no Battle of Britain then, and for the simple reason that the pass had previously been sold by Edward Heath under cover of a flaming lie that no surrender of substantial sovereignty was involved. When Churchill wished to commit our fighter squadrons to the Battle of France Dowding, at a grave cost to his own career, was able to restrain him. Submerged in the European Economic Community we should have no such choice — the decision would lie in the hands of the Communist-orientated directors of international financial policy.

Even so, vitally important though our defence problem undoubtedly is, important though the position of sterling, the marketing of New Zealand produce, the need to safe-guard Caribbean sugar and other such matters unquestionably are, yet in a very real sense they are of secondary importance when ranged beside the appalling fact that what is contemplated and imminent is nothing less than the suicide of Great Britain and with it the destruction, root and branch, of the entire British world altogether beyond the power of man to rebuild. And this act, I insist, is treason and would still be treason even if the bulk of the British people were to be hoodwinked into acquiescence. There is such a thing as a duty to the British past and an even greater to the British future. The man who would sell — or chuck away our splendid British nation into the stews of cosmopolitan servitude deserves a noose around his neck.

Although Britain's manhood nominally fought the first war "to save poor little Belgium" (which incidental aim was achieved) in reality, once the struggle began, they were fighting for their own national survival and the survival of the British world across the seas. If in the second world war they were fighting for the sovereign independence of Poland, then such was their failure that VE-Day should have been a day of national mourning. In truth, of course, once the war had been provoked they were again fighting for their own national survival and for that of the British world beyond the seas, and once again triumph crowned their magnificent qualities.

Of what conceivable use was all the blood-letting and all the untold and untellable agony of these two world-shattering events, for what long-term purpose were the superb qualities of our fighting-men enlisted, if the result in the life-time of many of us was to be the handing of our realm into the clutches of Rothschild Freres, former chief executive and his like by a bunch of political flaneurs, chancers and general light-weights indifferent to the proud traditions of the British race and to all else except keeping step with the beat of the Wall-street drum. Should they have their way, then in the name of decency let them recover whatever may remain of the bodies of John Amery and William Joyce, that they may be buried in Westminster Abbey and be duly canonized as the pioneers who blazed the path into Europe for Edward Heath and his accomplices.

II

CHAMPAGNE OR THE ROPE

By A. K. CHESTERTON

Candour # 512, July 1971.

AS has been noted before in these pages, the House of Commons seems to exude a vitiating atmosphere that politically emasculates most of its members, turning them into political zombies or mere lobby-fodder, which is much the same thing. One by one throughout the years I have seen Parliamentary White Hopes, champions of the British future, succumb to the contagion and become political eunuchs, cringing at the crack of the Party Whips and obedient servitors of the masters who for the last quarter of a century have been selling a once proud and mighty nation down the River Thames. The effect of the atmosphere on those who achieve Ministerial or Shadow-Ministerial rank is still more disturbing. If it does not actually corrupt them, as sometimes happens, it almost always reveals and highlights the defects of character which cause them to embrace even the most deplorable expedients as though they were immortal principles indeed, the prominence accorded them only enhances their pitiful inadequacy for the work entrusted to their care.

* * * *

As instances, if Anthony Eden had been content with **his own metier he would have filled with grace and distinction** the Chair of Arabic at one of our great universities: instead, his irrational ambition led him to become a light-weight Foreign Secretary in a very tough world and subsequently the fatuous Prime Minister who brought upon his country the disgrace of its belly-crawl from Suez. Eden the flaneur gave way to Harold Macmillan the dilettante, who would have done less harm had he stayed with the publishing company which bears his name and where his undoubted gifts and self-regard would have found an outlet better suited to his particular talent. Of the long succession of comic-opera Prime Ministers Douglas Home has the strongest claim upon our indulgence in that for the role of Coco the Clown he is to the manner born. Worse was to come. Harold Wilson had no need to write *Our Years In Power* to convince realists that his stewardship of our national destiny was that of a bouncing Narcissus, a feather-weight who knows no patriotism, whose knowledge of world affairs is at best half-baked, and whose opportunism is so irresponsible that his every statement has to be treated with reserve. After alienating the loyal Rhodesians, his one tawdry "achievement", Wilson was given the boot and we now find ourselves saddled with a very different kind of Prime Minister.

I once described Edward Heath as having all the fire and sparkle of a cold rice pudding and I am of the same opinion still. It was legitimate, however, to suppose, reversing the aphorism, that he would have the qualities of his defects — that he would be found to possess a rough and ready, if not perhaps a very articulate, fondness for the truth. In his private life this is almost certainly the fact. I do not think that as a private citizen he would find it easy to tell lies. But in his political life, conditioned by the toxic atmosphere of the House of Commons and even more by the heady wine of Premiership — what a difference! And for Great Britain how tragic that difference may prove to be!

* * * *

Last month, when Edward Heath declared that adherence to the Common Market would not entail any substantial erosion of Britain's sovereignty; I wasted no time in searching for polite euphemisms but told the man that what he said was a downright lie. Several readers sent that issue of *Candour* to Downing Street and it may be that he read it. Whether that is so or not, Heath has several times repeated the lie as though repetition by some magic contrivance could turn it into truth.

To find authority for *Candour's* challenge it is not even necessary to refer to The Treaty of Rome, with all its cast-iron provisions. During the negotiations in Brussels and Luxembourg, Heath's Super-Politico-Grocer, the man with the wooden smile and podgy insensitive face which by now must induce nausea in all television viewers, had to secure foreign accord about such matters as our coal and steel industries, while agreeing to a 20 per cent decrease in butter imports from New Zealand, our loyal daughter-nation, and to a fixed price based on the average of the past four years in a situation of wild world-wide inflation, to withdraw sterling as an international currency and to phase out almost every other form of control over Britain's economic, fiscal and legal systems. If these things do not betoken the erosion of national sovereignty, what the hell does?

I say once again, with all the emphasis in my power, that Edward Heath lies and that to lie on such an issue, which involves the very existence of our British identity and the cohesion of all that we have helped to build across the seas, is to participate in an act of constructive treason which in a healthier time would have called for the services of the public hangman.

But not the gallows for Edward Heath, rather an eventual peerage of the Realm he seeks to destroy; for Geoffrey Rippon[3] not the noose but the champagne which he guzzled at Luxembourg to celebrate his victory in preparing to do for his country that which no foreign power has succeeded in doing since the year 1066.

---

[3] **Aubrey Geoffrey Frederick Rippon,** (1924–1997) was the British Conservative politician who negotiated Britain's entry to the Common Market.

* * * *

Where Parliament does not warp character, it still has power to distort it, as with Enoch Powell. Ten years ago, together with his boss at the Treasury, the now ennobled Peter Thorneycroft, he backed Macmillan's European free trade area scheme which allowed for our adhering economically to the Common Market, while rejecting the provisions of the Treaty of Rome. It is surprising that a man of Powell's altogether remarkable intellect failed to understand that relinquishment of fiscal control inevitably carried with it control over our political future. Only today, when the crazed leadership of the party he supports has accepted the Treaty of Rome with all its implications, has he awakened to the deadly threat to our national survival which confronts us, but perhaps because of the fog permeating the House of Commons he makes the grave mistake of assuming that the British people have experienced a similar awakening. Indeed, he has congratulated them on the instinct for self-preservation which he believes to have led them to take up their anti-Common Market stance. It is true that they do possess this instinct, but it is quite untrue that it has become activated by the intrigues in Paris, Brussels and Luxembourg. Probably not one in fifty has ever heard of the Treaty of Rome and not one in a thousand has read into it the great plot against national sovereignty. Instead, as the public opinion polls reveal, British opponents of the E.E.C. merger base their case on the increase in the cost of living which would follow, which is simply not good enough.

* * * *

That we live in an age of grasping materialism does not need to be stressed, but something infinitely more precious than material values is here involved. As man does not live by bread alone, so do great nations not sustain themselves by balancing the price of a loaf against the promise of an increase in the weekly pay-package. Butter, cheese, sugar, fishing rights, the role of sterling and all such matters are important within their own contexts, but those contexts can only be seen in perspective when placed beside the transcendental unity created by upwards of a thousand years of common effort embracing both the exhilaration of success and the shared anguish of disaster.

In other words, what is being traded or recklessly flung away is the spirit of the British nation — a spirit tempered by a millennium of historical endeavour. The materialists in the avidity of their lust for the porcine slopes will dismiss this fact as sentimental, but without sentiment, which is the main-spring of all arts and crafts and of the will to excel, life would be reduced to mere biological functioning, a squalid non-experience which would find its only decency in death. Whatever the internal strains and stresses, whatever the contradictions and antagonisms, whatever the justice and the injustice, whatever the high aspiration and the low intent, there has been created the British soul, which binds in "togetherness" Britons the world over and gives them the pride of "belonging" —the only pride that confers true stature. Lacking it, men are fit only for nothingness, or — what is worse — for the purulence of decay.

* * * *

In two world wars the Anzacs, the Canadians, the South Africans, the Rhodesians, the Highland Division, the Guards Division, the men of the grand old county regiments, our superb seamen and victors in the air, did not give their lives by hundreds of thousands on behalf of the price of bread, the amount of the pay packet, ratios of sugar or butter, fishing limits, the role of sterling or any other of the matters now the subject of negotiation. Important though they be, these matters do not inspire men to sacrifice their lives: only the compulsion to safe-guard and hand down to posterity the splendour of the British spirit had that vital power. Is it conceivable that in swilling the champagne provided by his Luxembourg hosts Geoffrey Rippon spared a solitary minute from his orgy of self-congratulation to think upon the warrior dead of the British Empire?

So toxic is the atmosphere of the House of Commons, if any Member were brave enough to voice his opposition to the Common Market on the basis of defending the soul of Britain he would be howled down by the yahoos of all three parties. Yet in truth is this not the only factor? I ask the question not as a romantic but as a realist. To prove me wrong it would be necessary to establish that in my own life-time one million and a half Britons died on the battlefield on behalf of butter, sterling, fishing limits or some prophetic image of Edward Heath's fixed smile.

The way out for M.P.s who might be expected to show concern is to deny, as Heath has done, that the question of sovereignty is at issue. Typical of the simplistic arguments which they use was Sir Tufton Beamish's statement that, the Common Market notwithstanding, France was still France, Germany still Germany, Italy still Italy and so on. The truth of the gallant knight's utterance is incontrovertible, but it loses all force when placed beside the fact that not only is England still England, Scotland still Scotland, Wigan still Wigan and Hampstead Heath still Hampstead Heath but that Czechoslovakia is still Czechoslovakia, Poland still Poland and Hungary still Hungary. That Parliamentarians' puerilities should be accorded the power of throwing a thousand years of history into the discard is appalling beyond the range of words to describe.

Nor does the idea of a plebiscite inspire much greater confidence, in that the people's own money is at the disposal of the Government wherewith to beguile the people and cause them to betray their past and obliterate their future as a self-controlling national organism. The extent of the risk is revealed by Little Jack Horner Rippon when he appears on television to depict the rich opportunities of the free access of fifty-five million people to a market of two hundred and fifty million people, with never a word about the vulnerability of a market of fifty-five million to the inroads upon their economy which must be made by the free access accorded the mass-produced exports of the two hundred and fifty million. Rippon and Heath are no amateurs in the game of moulding public opinion and they would never stress the benefits of a one-way traffic if they had the least fear that their opponents possessed adequate means of countering that claim by stressing the far greater disadvantages of the adverse balance which must be created by a two-way traffic. It is not in the role of benefactor that Rothschild Freres of Paris have acquired a sky-scraper in the London area, but in the role of hawk.

Bearing in mind these considerations and the fluctuations revealed in opinion polls, it is difficult to place much more reliance through a referendum on the British people than one does on their Parliamentary representatives. If they remain convinced that adherence to the E.E.C. will hit them in their pockets, then no doubt the right decision given for the less worthy reason is preferable to the wrong decision. But it will not for long avail. Unless the British people rediscover their sense of history, their national soul and their identity with their kinsmen overseas, sooner rather than later they will be delivered like trussed fowl to the awaiting financial hawks of cosmopolis.

Should the day of awakening dawn, the laboured smile will be swiped from the face of Edward Heath and the Rippon glass will be empty of champagne.

III
HELL-BENT FOR THE DARK

By A. K. CHESTERTON

Candour # 513, August 1971.

WHEN the barbarians — accurately to be defined as strangers without the gate — were poised for the final sweep on Rome, their task was facilitated by the activities of the strangers within the gate who had infiltrated the bureaucracy while others served as foreign legionaries; beneath the Roman eagle. The imperial city itself had become a cosmopolitan stew wherein treachery and decay established so absolute a masterdom that still untainted citizens, faithful to her high traditions and dedicated to her survival, found that they were not so much fighting her enemies as drawing swords against a purulent disease. Even so, the manner in which Rome fell, although in all conscience foul enough, might be thought preferable to the death of Britain as the end product of perhaps the smoothest, the slickest and the most gigantic public relations job that this country has ever known.

* * * *

No blue-print was drawn up for the destruction of Rome. For the destruction of Britain through adherence to the Common Market large sums of public money have been used to publish a Government White Paper which, so far from being a statement of facts, reads like a fraudulent prospectus offering the British people shares in a millennium glittering beyond the boundaries of the most ecstatic opium-induced vision. To put across this quite fantastic confidence trick, Prime Minister Heath has managed to lay aside his podgy, pedestrian image and become animated with a super-charged missionary zeal. Even his very voice has been divorced from its former somnolence and approaches ever nearer to the sugary persuasiveness of soft-sell commercial television: "You'll be **comfortable** in the Common Market. The Common Market really **works**. The Common Market will make Britain **great** again." So the voices purr on and on and on.

The Heath arguments match the new Heath style. To persuade is his sole intent. One day he affirms that our economic weakness requires that we join the Common Market. The next day, answering a criticism, he asserts that what enables us to join is the sheer strength of our economy. If the truth should happen to get in the way of the new Heath dynamism, so much the worse for the truth. It gets stood on its head. The real measure of the man's obsession, however, is his brazen argument that because of the enormous importance of the decision that has to be taken it would not be reasonable for the Government to allow a free vote in the House of Commons. The fatuous gathering of Conservative yes-men and yes-women who heard him make this statement in the Central Hall, Westminster, greeted it with tumultuous applause, the measure of their mental capacity! If ever there were a vital issue demanding the non-intervention of the Party Whips, it is surely the issue raised by adherence to the Treaty of Rome, a step which by curtailing national sovereignty from the outset and eventually phasing it out to make way for an overriding European authority would be not so much to place our national future at risk as to ensure that there was no national future to be risked. To bring pressure to bear on Members of Parliament demanding that they place Britain in such mortal peril is intolerable — an adventure in political immorality of the wickedest, the most despicable kind.

The reply of Edward Heath and the other Ministers of The Great Decadence is to deny that the Treaty of Rome will cause any substantial erosion of sovereignty. They would have us believe, in other words, that the Treaty does not mean what its provisions explicitly state that it means. To prove that they are men of truth it would be necessary for the Prime Minister and his colleagues to establish that the Treaty of Rome does not require the free movement of goods and capital across national frontiers, that it does not call for the co-ordination of municipal laws, that the E.E.C. bureaucracy is not free to operate outside the control of national parliaments, that its edicts are not automatically binding on member states, that there is no sharing of usufruct and that Frenchmen, Germans, Italians and the rest will not have as much right to work, residence and ownership in the United, Kingdom as native Britons enjoy. Since such proof cannot be adduced, the men who seek to mislead us would seem, to have no alternative in logic other than to suggest that the drafting of the Treaty was only a parlour-game to, keep the drafters amused. Preposterous though the suggestion be, Heath need only to put it forward for his witless followers to give him loud and prolonged applause.

Into this phantasmagoria comes tumbling Conservatism's most egregious clown, the Lord Chancellor, who dons and doffs and dons again his title of nobility in the course of political job-hunting and whose mastery of legerdemain has led him to bring a touch of comic opera into the Government's otherwise squalid conspiracy of deception. What his quasi-legal thinking on the subject produces is the quaint idea that so far from Britain's abrogating her sovereignty, in fact through adherence to the Treaty of Rome it will be greatly extended. This half-baked idea is derived from her proposed acquisition of a voice in the councils of the European authority. How false is the argument can be shown by a simple analogy. The man who runs his own business is his own master. If he and the owners of six other businesses decide upon a merger to form a single company, he will doubtless be given a seat on a board of seven directors and therefore a share of one-seventh in the policy-making of the new concern.

To pretend that thereby he gains increase of sovereignty is to make nonsense of words. In that he can be out-voted by six to one he is no longer sovereign. Even should he be given a power of veto, the exercise of a one-man veto must make a nonsense of business. On a multi-national basis, as in the E.E.C., the power of veto is itself limited by the independent powers invested in the bureaucratic cabal in Brussels. Does Lord Hailsham understand the words he uses? Is he a political schizophrenic or can he be written off as a not too scrupulous political humbug? Hailsham's semantic flounderings are matched by flounderings of Heath in the historical field. Presenting the European Community as a means of keeping the peace, the Prime Minister announced in scholarly tones that the task was to heal the breach in Europe caused twelve hundred years ago. What an era in which to search for peace and comity! The reference, beyond doubt, was to the Holy Roman Empire, and in particular to the times of Charles the Great. That the Emperor deserved his title is not denied, but neither can it be denied that it was earned entirely by his military prowess. When Charles was not fighting the Saxons he was fighting the Slavs, or the Lombards, or the Westphalians or the Bavarians or the Spaniards. His war against the Saxons ran into no less than fourteen campaigns. When there was no war to be waged, there were raids to be repelled or uprisings to be suppressed. Indeed, the whole Charlemagne opos was of battle, culminating in the famous defeat at Roncesvalles. Now Edward the Great would inherit the mantle of Charles the Great. It is true that the new pretender does not think in terms of war. It is an even more significant truth that Europe twelve hundred years ago was struggling and sweating through the millennium known as the Dark Ages to which the benighted Edward

Heath, in a fine unhistorical frenzy and all unknowingly calls upon us to return.

The somewhat sick humour of the Prime Minister's mediaeval posturing is not present in the rest of his case. Mostly it consists of unrelieved deception. Here is an almost classic example of his use of *the suppresso veri suggestio falsi techniques*. I quote a passage from his Central Hall address:

"It is suggested we should build up the Commonwealth into a highly protected area. But they don't want a common political policy or defence policy or trading policy. Far from building up a Commonwealth preferential area we have seen since 1958 that gradually this preferential area has been eroded. They want to make their own arrangements."

Heath added that what encouraged the Commonwealth countries to find other outlets for their trade were the provisions of the General Agreement on Tariffs and Trade, but as the Treaty was concluded at Geneva in 1947 it is permissible to ask him why they should have waited for eleven years before taking advantage of the alleged benefits. The truth, which he shamelessly suppresses, is that throughout this period our daughter nations over and over again made known the great value they placed upon the Imperial preference system. Diefenbaker even won an election on the strength of a promise, subsequently dishonoured to switch 22 1/2 per cent of Canada's trade with the United States to the United Kingdom.

* * * *

What caused these countries after 1958 to seek alternative outlets was not any reliance placed on the General Agreement, but despair induced by the determined attempts of the Macmillan Government to establish a free trade area with Europe, which would provide for Continental goods to enter Britain duty-free while theirs would be obliged to jump a tariff wall. During my speaking-tour of New Zealand and Australia in 1960 1 received first-hand information about Australian trade commission's travelling all over Asia in search of markets against the day when they would encounter barriers at the British ports. The price to be paid, as they knew, would be a heavy one. Markets are not made available without reciprocal benefits and already Japan has not only acquired substantial assets in both countries but begun to exert political pressure on such vital matters as the White Australian policy. Anzacs knew the risks they ran but felt that they had no other option, sensing that sooner or later a British Government would ditch the Imperial Preference system and leave them to sink or swim. Apart from a temporary life-buoy flung to New Zealand, the Rt. Hon. Edward Heath, showing an obsessive zeal and exuberance hitherto unsuspected, is hell-bent upon proving their instinct sound. And lying like a cheap watch in the process.

If those who drew up or approved the White Paper had even the smallest particle of political honour they would have ensured that it did not read like a rose-tinted travel brochure. They would have set down what they believe to be the "pros" on the one side and an objective statement of the "cons" on the other, thereby giving the British public a chance of deciding upon their destiny without benefit of confidence tricksters breathing down their backs to falsify the facts and stampede them with the high-powered propaganda into making an irrevocable act of national slaughter. As they have not done so I will attempt as briefly as possible to act in their default.

(1) The problem of sovereign independence has already been discussed. All that remains under this heading is to ask the Prime Minister how he would answer President Pompidou's unequivocal assertion that if Britain wished to enter the European Community "she must make a complete break with her identity."

(2) Entering Continental Europe can only further the P.E.P. Chatham House scheme of inter-national industrial and commercial mergers as an essential feature of the drive towards ever-expanding monopoly. The terms of life will be made increasingly difficult, and in the final phase impossible, for the small man and the small company everywhere.

(3) What would be the difference between an economy dominated by giant monopolies and the Soviet economy? Is it not certain that the political implications would become the same for both?

(4) In the meantime it has to be remembered that while the Communist Party in Britain is small, the French and Italian Communist parties are powerful. The free movement of labour across national frontiers must inevitably include the free movement of Communist agitators.

(5) Although most British trade unions are now against entry, once entry is effected trade unionism here will before long seek federation with trade unionism in Europe, thereby multiplying beyond calculation strike action and general industrial unrest. Will they be eased by the more temperate British approach or will the British approach be influenced by Italian amok-runs? The answer to this question should take into account that Italy's rudimentary social welfare services will hold no attraction for British workers, whereas our own highly developed services will attract Italian workers by the hundreds of thousands to come swarming into Britain.

(6) Relative to points 4 and 5, the prospect of British miners or railwaymen or motor-car workers downing tools in sympathy with their counterparts in France or Germany or Holland or Italy or wherever can scarcely be more pleasurable than the prospect of polyglot rabbles rampaging down Whitehall to make political protests on issues remote from our own shores.

(7) Relative to points 4, 5 and 6, it is a moot point as to which would pose the greater threat to society —European Monopoly Capitalism or European Monopoly Trade Unionism.

(8) Leaving present frenzies out of account, even under the most peaceful dispensation the opening up of Britain to all corners must intensify the problems already created by coloured immigration, leading to a further watering down of our native British stock and the inexorable erosion of British values and traditions.

(9) What was heralded as the Great Debate has proved to be a series of endless petty squabbles about possible economic advantages and disadvantages, in the course of which the Government's chief claim has escaped investigation. The claim, as put forward in the White Paper reads:

"In the light of the experience of the Six themselves, and their conviction that the creation of the Community materially contributed to their growth, and of the essential similarity of our economies, the Government are confident that membership of the enlarged Community will lead to much improved efficiency and productivity in British industry, with a higher rate of investment and a faster growth of real wages."

The "essential similarity of our economies" — that is, or should be, the crux of the argument. Great Britain is a heavily over-industrialised country, dependent for her very life upon the importation of foodstuffs and raw materials. Sanity demands that she should co-operate ever more closely with complementary economies able to supply these needs, whereas the Imperial Preference system which guaranteed them is being thrown overboard in favour of the European tie-up. This is not only the gravest general disservice to Britain and her former overseas partners; it must also — whatever the farming interests may assert deal a lethal blow to British agriculture. And for this reason. The former system provided preferences to overseas producers but not the right of free entry. Thus protection could be given to home producers, whereas after transitional periods have expired there will be no protection against the duty-free entry of foreign produce not only from the Common Market countries but also from Greece, Turkey, Tunisia, Morocco, Spain and Israel, with whom they have made preferential agreements. That Britain should also undertake to give preferences to these countries while denying them to Australia, Canada and South Africa maketh the heart sick. It has also to be remembered that France retains a large peasant economy against which in free trade conditions British farmers cannot hope to compete, even on the home market.

(10) As the British Government's claim in the economic field is shown to be bogus, so is its alleged political motivation. This, stated briefly, is that the Community will make Europe independent of the so-called Super-Powers, and better able to compete with them for world markets. It is not in the nature of things for nations, whether or not they be "super-powers" to welcome strong competition. Yet the United States has given every encouragement to the creation of the Common Market and used its utmost endeavours to bulldoze Great Britain into full Community membership. Indeed, ten years ago the late President Kennedy, reinforcing the stand made by Professor Hallstein, then Secretary-General of the E.E.C., stated that Britain in joining the Common Market would be **required** to accept the provisions of the Treaty of Rome. After the recent Luxembourg conference President Nixon sent telegrams of congratulation to Edward Heath and the heads of the other participating governments. Do such actions suggest pure altruism in American hearts? Or is it not much more probable that Wall Street sees in the enlarged community, not a cut-throat competitor, but an economic colony which it will dominate and use for its own ends?

(11) Israel Moses Sieff's Political and Economical Planning has joined forces with Chatham House (the British equivalent of the Council of

Foreign Relations) to flood the country with pro-Market propaganda. As the policies which these bodies incubated during the 'thirties, 'forties and 'sixties had a strange habit of being incorporated in legislation, it is perhaps highly significant that their latest treatise envisages the extension of the European Economic Community to embrace the Soviet Union and its satellites. Those who study the subterranean conspiracies which shape the pattern of human affairs are aware that international financiers in New York found the money for the Russian revolutions in 1917 and that close liaison has ever since been maintained between the dominant Money Power and the Communist Empire. It was to be foreseen that sooner rather than later there would be launched a campaign to bring the Soviet Union into the whole of Europe as it was brought at Yalta into the European heartlands. The final objective is a One-World tyranny. The Heaths, the Rippons, the Maudlings, the Hoggs and the rest may suppose that they bestride the European stage as statesmen of the highest order, but in truth they are being used as mere puppets by the masters of mankind.

The only hope lies in the full awakening of the British instinct for survival to the menace of what portends. Should they come to their senses in time it will be more than possible for them to prevent what has been miscalled The Great Debate from becoming The Great Debacle. They have but to assert the British will to live a resurgent British life for their declaration to bring a vast new hope to their kinsmen in the far corners of the earth and from that hope will come a vibrant and life-giving response. To nurture the belief that British communities of nearly a hundred million people, strategically placed around the world and possessing everything needful for their sustenance, cannot shape for themselves a destiny far more splendid than any foreign association can offer is to be guilty of wilful blindness, defeatism — and, often enough, downright treason.

The decision is one for us alone to decide. If we fail to rise to the level of our potentiality, if we allow our petty politicos to lead us into the European wilderness, there will be nothing left for us to say to Britannia other than the lines has spoke to her royal mistress:

"Finish, good lady; the bright day is done,

And we are for the dark."

IV

U.S. BULLDOZING BRITAIN INTO EUROPE

By A. K. CHESTERTON

Candour # 514, September 1971.

THE march towards World Government has many approach lines. When one becomes blocked the wide boys of international finance in Wall Street, with their affiliates elsewhere are quick to find alternative routes. For instance, in the late 'thirties the Atlantic Union scheme to unite the countries on the Atlantic sea-board within a federal structure came to grief because of the isolationist attitude then prevailing in the United States. Far from being disheartened, the internationalist policy-makers next determined to start with the unification of Europe and their first step was most encouraging to them. The coal, steel and iron industries of France and Germany were wedded in accordance with the so-called Schumann Plan — a name which tactfully concealed the fact that it was designed by David Lilienthal, progenitor of the dubious Tennessee Valley project.

* * * *

Sights were then raised for an all-out attempt to secure the political unification of Europe through the Strasbourg movement, but when this venture failed to get off the ground the internationalists placed it in mothballs (if Lord Boothby and Mr. Christopher Hollis will forgive the metaphor) and proceeded at once to seek political federation by hiding their intentions under the economic cover. Thus was born the Common Market and with it the European Economic Community, based on the enactments of the Treaty of Rome. The political motivation was now all too clear. When Harold Macmillan endeavoured to secure Britain's adherence to the Common Market, by-passing its political implications, he was promptly slapped-down by Professor Hallstein, the E.E.C.'s chief functionary, at the same time as President Kennedy stipulated that Great Britain would only be admitted to the Common Market if she subscribed to the provisions of the Treaty of Rome in their entirety. As Kennedy could not have been speaking in his role of President, in that the United States had no conceivable right to meddle in the affairs of sovereign nations, one is justified in assuming that he spoke as a ventriloquist's dummy manipulated by the Money Power. In fact all the evidence available establishes that the European Common Market is the child of High Finance, and that Britain's entry into the E.E.C. is required as a further step towards the obliteration of nationhood and its replacement by the phased advance to World Government.

These moves are all part of the conspiracy which dominates our century and threatens to destroy all our most dearly prized values. As I have written elsewhere it is more often than not impossible to name the conspirators, the essence of a conspiracy being that it is plotted in secrecy, far from the public gaze. Nor is the naming of them important once one finds that all the highways and by-ways lead inexorably to the same political objective. By their policies shall you know them.

*　*　*　*

There are, however, incidental clues which throw light on the fact of conspiracy. If the principals, such as the late Bernard Baruch, cannot always be tracked down, their agents — having to do much of their work in public — are unable to enjoy the same concealment and it is they who often let the cat out of the bag. Let us look at one or two of them within the context of the stampede to drown Britain's sovereignty in the Common Market cesspool. To possess significance, they must have worked in the top echelons of what can most conveniently and accurately be called the Internationalist Bureaucracy, of whom the prototype was the late Adlai Stevenson. Dean Acheson and George Ball are as representative of the species as any now alive.

One night last month the B.B.C. allowed a full hour on television to an interview with Acheson, who laid on the charm with a trowel. No awkward question was fired at him to disturb the even tenor of the occasion. He was not asked to explain why, after two juries had found Alger Hiss guilty of perjury in denying that he was a Communist agent within the U.S. Government apparatus, he reaffirmed his friendship with the traitor. Nor was mention made of Acheson's strangely gratuitous pronouncement as Secretary of State that Korea lay outside the bounds of the U.S. defence zone — a clear invitation which the North Koreans were swift to accept. No less curious was the fact that the Soviet Union at that time was withholding the light of its presence from the Security Council, so that its power of veto need not be invoked. As in many other matters Wall Street, the State Department and the Kremlin were playing footy-footy under the table in pursuit of an agreed policy.

After about forty-five minutes of the television interview one began to wonder why so much time was being given to the build-up of the Acheson charm and his retailing of light gossip about the great and the not-so-great, the inevitable happened. "Mr. Acheson", said the interviewer, "you have been quoted as saying that Britain has lost an empire and has yet to find a role. Is that still your opinion?" Then the Acheson voice at last became serious and incisive. "No", he replied, "Britain has now found a role — to enter the Common Market and take the lead in Europe". Here was the heart of the matter. Whether or not the former Secretary of State and avowed friend of Alger Hiss was flown across the Atlantic expressly to say his piece I have no means of ascertaining but it is enough to know that the B.B.C. gave him an hour on the air to recognise the importance attached to the interview.

* * * *

George W. Ball, former Assistant Secretary of State and, like Acheson, a Bilderberger and member of the Council of Foreign Relations, was also brought into the arena to testify to the Wall Street decision at all costs to hurl Great Britain into the European Economic Community. I do not know whether the B.B.C. has yet grabbed Ball for a television interview, but the chance is unlikely to be missed. Meanwhile he was offered by *The Times*, and accepted, an opportunity to set forth his views at length on Britain's entry into the Common Market. Here are his two opening paragraphs:

"We Americans are watching Britain's agony over Europe with far more intensity than our silence would suggest. Though an habitually noisy nation we are being studiously discreet since, sensitive to the charge of outspokenness in the past, we are determined not to create any false issues that might this time impede an affirmative decision. Yet it would be a major error to assume that we regard the matter with indifference; on the contrary, this is a time of mixed hope and anxiety when, in the view of thoughtful Americans, the promise of a stable western system is being critically tested".

Well, well, if the intensity of America's interest is what George Ball declares it to be, one can only wonder what would happen if it laid aside its "studious discretion". An ultimatum?

* * * *

Pains have been taken by the British Government to gloss over the political implications of the Treaty of Rome and put over the "case" for Britain's entry in terms of alleged economic advantage. Ball on the other hand writes that Americans "tend to focus more on the political than on the purely economic implications of the Rome Treaty", which is readily understandable in the light of projected World Government. But that does not preclude his dwelling on the "purely" (sic) economic advantage to be derived (by the United States!) from our adherence to the Common Market. I have mentioned above the tendency of the internationalist bureaucracy to let the cat out of the bag, and this is precisely what George Ball proceeds to do. I quote again:

"American business knows from its own experience that the Common Market has generated far more trade than it has deflected and taking account of the fact that United States exports to the Six have increased several fold since the Community first came into being they expect a further expansion of economic activity from British entry. Thus dozens of United States companies are waiting only for the final decision before regrouping their European operations under head offices in London —the city that will, as they see it, emerge as not only the financial but the commercial capital of the new and larger Europe".

This, with submission, reveals to the public gaze the entire short term motivation of the conspiracy. Even if London does become the financial and commercial capital of Europe and that is by no means certain, it will function only as an advance base for New York.

Britain's adherence to the Treaty of Rome would offer tremendous advantages to the wolf packs of Wall Street, who—as Ball informs us—are even now lining up in battle array to make the most of their opportunity. When the process is complete the New York Money Power, instead of having to bring pressure to bear on several national governments, will need to apply the carrot and the stick only to a single European authority.

* * * *

The other aims, although incidental, are not unimportant. Britain will serve as a bridgehead for the American monopolists in Europe, and at the same time Britain's final abandonment of her overseas relations will facilitate the American takeover which has been progressively stepped up ever since the last war. Not, of course, that Ball would commit such trifles to paper, even in so unsophisticated a journal as *The Times*. He prefers flattery to fact, as is made apparent in the two reasons he puts forward for our entry. One is that Britain's "political genius" is needed to make the European institutions work. As there has been no sign of such genius at any time during the present century, which politically—as distinct from militarily—has been one long retreat from greatness, it is clear that George Ball either admires the politics of defeat or simply does not know the score.

The second reason is that Western Germany, "shaking off the inhibitions of her war guilt" is "moving with confidence, though good faith, towards an independent and assertive foreign policy" so that in French eyes "the counterweight of Britain's commanding presence" will prevent the spectre of German predominance from again driving Europe "toward fragmentation and futility". This is truly an amazing argument. Germany is seen by Ball as a continuing menace: therefore, he argues, Britain should enter into partnership with her to redress the balance in the European Community. I do not for one moment accept the Ball view of Germany as a potential enemy, but if one assumed its validity the integration of our economy with that of Germany, the sharing of our military, scientific and industrial secrets, the joint production of projects (such as the partnership with France in building the Concord) would be acts of the sheerest lunacy. The man in danger of assassination does not set up house with the would-be assassin and make him privy to the details of his life; on the contrary, he keeps him at arm's length and sees to his own protection. I am here endeavouring to demolish the specious Ball argument, not advocating the treatment of Germany as a pariah. What I have in mind is George Washington's little known dictum that nothing is more foolish than to expect real favours to be bestowed by one nation on another.

* * * *

George Ball concludes his tendentious article with some-thing very much like a threat. He writes:

"For Britain to reject the brave chance now offered would be regarded in my country as a fatal sign of exhaustion and resignation - one more proof that Europe can never be a serious partner, one more excuse for Americans to turn their backs on a continent that seems incapable of organizing itself to meet the requirements of the modern age. I cannot believe that will happen".

Let Mr. Ball be reassured. Even if the instincts of the British people prevail, which at present does not seem probable, as long as there is a European power-mechanism to be operated or a dollar to he made in the European markets there will be no turning of American backs on the continent. This is a grave misfortune, in that Europe has been catastrophically weakened by the pressures brought to bear by New York and Washington on her national governments, most of all upon British governments, to surrender their overseas possessions in return for "aid" and to abort ventures which, if fully developed, could have made them increasingly independent of United States "protection". As examples, consider what happened to the T.S.R.2, Blue Streak and Black Arrow.

It would be a mistake to underestimate the significance of George Wildman Ball. Two partners in his law firm, which operates under different names in Washington and New York, were intimately involved in the United Nations racket which paved the way for the United States to usurp the authority over the Congo from which Belgium was ousted, and at the time Ball was Under-Secretary of State — a key position of vital importance in determining the

Congolese future. It was revealed not long afterwards that the law firm, using yet another name, was listed at the Justice Department of the U.S. as the agent for the Common Market, the European Coal and Steel Community and the European Atomic Energy Community. In writing his article for *The Times*, the former Assistant Secretary of State did not see fit to disclose his interest.

After leaving the State Department it was announced that George Ball was to work in conjunction with S. G. Warburg & Co. the London based firm of international financiers stemming from the notorious Kuhn, Loeb outfit. It was Sigmund Warburg who planned Wilson's withdrawal from East of Suez—a policy now carried out by Heath under cover of doing precisely the opposite). For some reason still to be discovered the Warburg-Ball motif has been played down and Ball is now presented to the world as an international financier in his own right, which seems highly improbable. The likelihood, amounting to a certainty, is that he is a front-man for the entire Wall Street complex.

* * * *

While Acheson and Ball choose —or are chosen— to take the stage in the role of propagandists, Wall Street bankers aspire to speak with a more authoritative voice, as did Mr. Harold Cleveland, president of the First National City Bank, when testifying to a Congressional committee. Here is part of his testimony:

"If Britain baulks, it will be on grounds of narrow economic nationalism and little Englandism on one side of the House of Commons, with a dash of imperial nostalgia thrown in from the other side. The act itself would tend to confirm and strengthen the negative trends in British thinking. An inward-looking passive Britain would be unable to play the role in European economic and political affairs which U.S. interests require Britain to play".

We need waste no time on the "Little Englander" taunt, which happens to be the one levelled by imperialists against the anti-Imperialists at the turn of the century. What cannot be disregarded is the statement that the United States, in service to its interests, **requires** us to enter Europe to further those interests. Could anything be more clearly stated? Will the several people who have written to tell me that my insistence that we are being pitch-forked into Europe by Wall Street banksterdom amounted to an obsession now make their apologies?

Not, indeed, that all the pressures came from across the Atlantic. Apart from the many American subsidiaries operating in Britain and therefore able to exert pressure from within, there is also a host of British combines, cartels, monopolies and near-monopolies anxious to seize the opportunity of joining their opposite numbers in Europe to make a corner in their own lines of business. The list of subscribers to the Royal Institute of Inter-national Affairs (which I have seen) embodies pretty well the whole shooting-match of finance houses, chain-stores and mammoth industrial corporations. Israel Moses Sieff's Political and Economic Planning receives support from much the same sources, and it is therefore no surprise that these two bodies should have come together to churn out pro-Market propaganda. The full-page advertisement in *The Times* signed by leading industrialists was only a pointer to the forces at work.

What, it may be asked, is their motivation? Leaving aside those tied to the Wall Street Money Power, it can only be ascribed to the lust of the monopolists to expand, expand, expand. The more they expand the stronger becomes their grip on national governments and inter-national authorities. The sinister reality was depicted in ecstatic tones by a writer in the *Daily Telegraph*, whose article concluded with these words:

"It is time to recognise that the multinational company, far from being a misfortune, is more in keeping with the needs of the present-day world than the national State. The political counter-point to the multinational company at present is the Common Market and at a later stage a free world economic order with a unified commercial law. The great mistake, as Prof. Harry Johnson has forcefully observed is to 'accept the rights of government to interfere with the operations of the corporation for its own frequently myopic and narrowly partisan purposes'."

All power to the Financial Capitalists!

This is the peril against which I have warned for over thirty years. Never did I think I would live to see it proclaimed as a positive benefit to be welcomed with open arms.

Moreover, to whet the greed of British-based monopolists, the E.E.C. Commission is now drawing up plans for the oil monopolies in the Common Market to merge into one gigantic monopoly which will enjoy special tax concessions. It also proposes to make available more money for the textile industries that they may "concentrate", in other words, establish a textile monopoly. Furthermore, it is to call for larger-scale assistance to the recently formed international merger of atomic power industries in the form of loans to the builders of atomic power stations.

These are some of the stark facts which account for the demoniacal energy with which the Heath-Rippon combination is bulldozing Britain into the Common Market. High (very high!) Finance and Big Business are bringing the most powerful pressures to bear in the devilish cause of destroying the nations of the world and replacing them with a world-embracing empire, with the World Emperor ensconced in Wall Street and ruling with the heads of the great monopolies as his viceroys, princes, dukes and barons. (The Presidents and Prime Ministers are already in the bag!). A tyrannical regime of this kind is the logical outcome of a human society which has allowed materialism to spread like a cancer throughout its very organism. Unless in the very near future we find antibodies to fight against this hideous social disease we shall die and our death will be well merited.

The first step, I submit, is ruthlessly to free ourselves from the clutches of the present cancer which is the New York Money Power. That accomplished, it will be a relatively easy job to deal with the Chatham House-P.E.P. secondaries.

Time is not on our side.

V

THIS FATEFUL YEAR

By A. K. CHESTERTON

Candour # 518, January 1972.

THROUGHOUT their history the British have shown themselves to be a very brave people, staunch in meeting their obligations, steadfast in claiming their rights and dauntless in repelling those who would steal from them their heritage. The one factor needed to bring these qualities to the fore has been the threat of visible peril.

Where the peril is invisible, cunningly devised by enemies (often enough their own leaders) who do not disclose their true aims, or who present them in a false light, then for the most part the British people, like most others, tend to be gullible and helpless, totally unfitted to defend their own interests. What defeats them is the decency which leads them to expect from those they trust the good faith in which they endeavour to live their own lives.

It is in no small part due to their exploitation of this trust that the politicians have been able to steer the British nation into a year of peril unsurpassed by any danger since the Norman Conquest. Indeed, because the Normans were soon assimilated and Anglicised, the danger today is infinitely greater than it was nine hundred years ago. If in 1972 we cannot bring pressure to bear upon the Government to reverse Parliament's iniquitous vote of last October, then on January 1, 1973, the British leaders will sign the Treaty of Rome—and, with it, Britain's death-warrant. The cosmopolitan architects of One World who are determined to be its dictators will have scored their greatest victory in the West to date.

* * * *

In the twelve months ahead the Government will be placing before Parliament hundreds of measures to obliterate or amend Britain's laws, customs and institutions so as to accord with what the European Economic Community requires of its members. Our own hope will be that by enlightening ever more of the general public we shall be able to help the anti-Common Marketeers in Parliament to muster support for the smashing of a sufficient number of the Government's proposals to make entry impossible.

One of our most important tasks will be to persuade good-natured Britons, who have been told by the Government that the object of merging the European nations is to secure peace and loving-kindness on a European scale, that such propaganda is as bogus as the deceitful Edward Heath's assurances that entry will not entail any erosion of our essential sovereignty.

* * * *

Here is the reality as depicted by Secretary of Trade and Industry, John Davies, in an address to a federal trust company in London: "It is important to create a climate in Europe that will allow companies to grow to their optimum size and efficiency. After Britain has joined the Common Market the Government will favour mergers to create some vast multi-national companies. It is necessary to match the giant corporations of the United States unless the future of the Common Market is to be jeopardised." If that be the truth of the matter, why have these giant U.S. Corporations all brought pressure to bear upon Britain to enter Europe? Why has one of New York's biggest bankers said that such entry is required in American interests? Mr. Davies really should explain.

I quote him further: "There are some very interesting proposals such as the use of the European investment bank, the introduction of

Community development contracts and wider use of the Euratom joint under-taking concept to assist cross-frontier collaboration. There are wide areas needing much further thought and action. Britain will have much to contribute."

It must have been at this stage that the realization came to the Secretary for Trade and Industry that not everyone who heard or would read his words had any desire whatever to belong to a gigantic multi-national monopoly, because a moment later came these words: "But I do not want to suggest that the interests of medium and small firms, which frequently play an important role in the innovative process should or will be overlooked." The intriguing question arises: not overlooked by whom?

I ask it because in another speech Mr. Davies uttered the surprising statement that henceforth the multi-national corporation would have more to offer mankind than the nation-state. Are we to suppose that from now on the small firm, seeking its modest place in the sun, will have to apply to a Europeanized I.C.I. or General Motors or General Electric for a licence to exist? If not, which particular authority will have the job of ensuring that this small firm in Bavaria or that small firm in South Wales will not be "overlooked"?

It seems to me clear enough that despite the woolly concern shown by Mr. Davies for the "little man", he is presenting himself as a strong proponent of Monopoly Capitalism and depicting the European Economic Community as its instrument. Had he been a little bolder, or perhaps a good deal more intellectually honest, he would not have tried to make out that European Monopoly is intended as a counter to American Monopoly but stated the plain truth that the real intention is an eventual merger of all mergers to form a One World Monopoly.

One of the greatest security chiefs in the West was once asked why so many Jews were attracted to Communism. His reply was important: "Because Communism is the most highly developed form of

Capitalism", he said. When Monopoly Capitalism through its various economic community projects grows to its full status it will have no less power over men's lives and liberties, thus removing any impediment to the marriage of East and West which will create One World.

* * * *

Ten years ago, speaking at a meeting in Cape Town, I said: "Unless we take guard, I see a time coming when the boast will be, not 'I am a citizen of no mean city' but 'I am a cog in no mean production unit'." Today the prediction seems less wild than it may have done at the time. Yet such a hideous future need not be ours. Nobody except the power-maniacs fail to shudder at the thought of it. If the British people can only shake themselves out of their state of coma within the next few months and force Parliament to reverse its criminally insane decision they may be able to deal this Devil's plan for One World a lethal blow.

* * * *

A million and a half Britons were not killed because they wished their historic country to come under European domination. What right have half-baked or unscrupulous politicians to make a mockery of those sacrifices by subjecting the nation to European overlordship? What voice directs them other than that of Big Brother in New York?

As *Candour* was the first periodical in the world to attack the concept of Great Britain's adherence to the Common Market, so shall we double and redouble our attacks in this fateful year. There is absolutely no effort we shall spare to prevent the murder of our nation and we trust that readers will go all out in our support. Should they fail to do so, should they give up the struggle at this decisive point, then our heavy labours of almost twenty years will have been but a futile dream.

We dismiss that thought and go ahead with full faith in our readership to do everything possible to help us save this country from becoming part of High Finance's most sordid bawdy-house. The bawdy-house which is called Cosmopolis.

VI

BRITAIN'S BLACKEST HOUR

By A. K. CHESTERTON

Candour # 519, February 1972.

ON Saturday, the twenty-second of January, nineteen hundred and seventy-two, Great Britain—in the lifetime of many of us the mightiest power on earth—was formally committed to the surrender of the scant remnants of that power, and with it her own freedom of action, to a cosmopolitan cabal excluded from allegiance to any nation. Present in Brussels to perform the ceremony was the British Prime Minister—to give him only three of his multilingual honorifics, the Right Honourable, Letzen Monat unterzeichnete, Seine Exzellenz, Le mois dernier le tres honorable Edward Heath.

It was in this cause that Heath had long devilled and at last the hour had come for him to enjoy his finest hour. The French Foreign Minister described the event as "among the most significant happenings in 1972"—a snide remark which doubtless made little if any dent in the man's leather-tough hide.

Much less subtle was the act of the woman who greeted his arrival at the Egmont Palace by throwing the contents of a bottle of black ink at him, which required him speedily to retire, wash, change his clothing and re-emerge with his plastic smile again in place to testify to the bulldog breed triumphing over every set-back.

Not even the most bitter of Heath's antagonists can approve this outlandish insult, but it is nevertheless impossible not to reflect upon its symbolism. Black in the English language is not a word expressing happiness. Men speak of "black looks". Our forefathers said to those who displeased them "The Devil damn thee black". Among other such usages it is the funereal colour.

* * * *

In this sense historians may remember the woman's black ink, however intended, as, proclaiming the death and impending burial of the historic British nation.

Edward Heath's signature to the Treaty of Accession in Brussels represented, not the will of the British people, but the culminating triumph of the mightiest display of power which High Finance and Big Business have ever exerted in the moulding of our country's destiny. Not one single banking, industrial or commercial vested interest dared to withstand the titanic pressures ruthlessly applied to bulldoze Britain's path to national extinction. When Harold Wilson headed the Government he was happy to serve as the minion of the Lords of Monopoly, and when he fell, the even more unscrupulous Heath, for long a hack enlisted in the cause, delightedly seized the opportunity to speed up the tempo of betrayal.

Had he and the political creatures who aided and abetted him been actuated by the faintest simulacrum of honest dealing, instead of using the taxpayers' money to produce a thoroughly misleading and tendentious document setting forth the alleged "advantages" of adherence to the Treaty of Rome, they would have made known the implications of the surrender to foreigners of British sovereignty. Failing to take the nation into his confidence, Heath went so far as to tell the House of Commons that there would be no erosion of essential sovereignty—perhaps the most brazen lie in Parliamentary history and without doubt the most audacious. The audacity lay in the fact that the provisions of the Treaty of Rome were available to shout "liar" to his face.

* * * *

While these provisions were known, what Parliament and the people had no means of knowing until almost the eve of Heath's signing the Treaty of Accession were the multitudinous regulations resulting from the Rippon and other negotiations, as also from the Rome enactment, which Parliament would be required to pass before Britain became a member of the European Economic Community. These measures demanded the harmonizing of her laws, fiscal policies, agricultural enactments and general procedures covering the entire field of her public life. Not the least important of the secondary issues were the standardizing of medical and educational qualifications. Only in the middle of January did Her Majesty's Stationery Office publish as much of the English-language text as had been agreed, but even this filled 42 volumes, containing thousands of items and running into millions of words. All the private citizen had .to do to master the contents was to pay a trifling £143 for the set and devote ten years or so to intensive study!

Members of Parliament, it is true, received free copies (of which the first sixteen volumes were at once distributed), but as there is no reason to suppose that more than a few of them had even troubled to read the enactments of the Treaty of Rome, little public good is likely to accrue from their possession of such massive material. This is no argument, of course, for Parliament to agree, as by a small majority it has agreed, to the signing of the Treaty of Accession before it knew precisely what adherence to the E.E.C. entailed. Only after signature will it be asked to pass the legislation needed to establish Britain as a fully-fledged member. What happens in the improbable event of that legislation proving too much to stomach and being refused?

* * * *

An easier question to answer is: "Why the frantic, almost obscene haste in rushing to sign the Treaty of Accession before its terms have been approved in legislative detail, instead of securing approval by January 1 next year?" The only reason which occurs to me is the slavering greed of the monopolists and their political hacks to get the treasonable package tied up neatly in advance.

Questioned on the subject in the Commons, Heath cited what had happened in the handling of previous treaties, as though what was now required had any precedent in British history. Here are his words: "We shall follow the British constitutional procedure of using the right of prerogative of the Crown as Her Majesty's Government to sign the Treaty of Accession on Saturday, January 22." (Conservative cheers.)

What the cheering dimwits failed to recognise was that Heath cited constitutional authority for the obliteration of the constitution and the Sovereign's title for the virtual elimination of the Queen's sovereignty. That, and nothing but that, is the long-term truth. So great a gift of duplicity deserves more than a £36,000 Toepper Prize for Statesmanship.

* * * *

When Harold Wilson was urging Britain's entry into the E.E.C. he argued that it meant "more and more Socialist controls". The Heath case is that it means more and more Capitalist controls. One remembers Rippon's cry: "Think European . . . Europeanisation of British Industry . . . bigger and bigger industrial giants cutting across national frontiers!" No less emphatic was the statement of Secretary of Trade and Industry, Davies: "It is important to create a climate in Europe that will allow companies to grow to their optimum size and efficiency. After Britain has joined the Common Market the Government will favour mergers to create some vast multi-national companies. It is necessary to match the giant corporations of the United States unless the future of the Common Market is to be jeopardised."

Does this mean that the Conservative and Labour approaches to Europe are fundamentally opposed? No such thing. What it does reveal is that in modern terms Capitalism and Socialism are blood-brothers and in the end result will appear before the world as inseparable as Siamese twins. The Davies' assertion of the need to match the giant U.S. corporations is the sheerest bluff. Were it otherwise those corporations would scarcely be in the vanguard of the forces driving Britain into Europe. As long ago as 1961 the late President Kennedy decreed that she should adhere to the Treaty of Rome. Ten years later President Nixon, as soon as agreement was reached, sent his congratulations to all concerned. We have shown in earlier numbers how George Wildman Ball and the late Dean Acheson, both agents of the Money Power, worked their stint to influence opinion in Britain and we have also quoted the view of Harold Cleveland, president of the First National Bank of New York that her failure to accept the whip must mean that "Britain would be unable to play the role in European economic affairs which U.S. interests require Britain to play".

* * * *

Furthermore, no sooner was the Brussels agreement reached than a London banking concern which acts as an industrial, financial and commercial marriage-broker distributed far and wide a prospectus announcing the formation of a consortium to promote mergers throughout the E.E.C. Stress was laid on the need to build up Europe's economic strength to enable her to compete on equal terms with the United States. The wealthiest component in this consortium was an American finance house with ramifications extending over the entire range of American business. The American giants would appear to have a very odd lust for competition.

* * * *

How many British Members of Parliament called attention to these matters? To the best of my knowledge not one. Either they cannot read the writing on the wall, or, having read it, are terrified to offend the masters of mankind by spelling it out. Thus do cowards join with traitors in the betrayal of their country.

What no enemy has been able to do throughout the centuries by force of arms is now about to be accomplished by the cosmopolitan slicksters who "fight by shuffling papers". Rather than suffer this ignominious defeat upon the altar of Monopoly, death in battle would have been infinitely preferable.

VII

OPEN LETTER TO EDWARD HEATH

By A. K. CHESTERTON

Candour # 520, March 1972.

SIR,

You gave the British people, whose interests you so disastrously misrepresent, the pledge that on no account would you take the United Kingdom into the European Economic Community unless you had their overwhelming consent and the overwhelming consent of Parliament.

In the strange new world which we inhabit words seem to have no meaning in their own right, so that it would be futile to consult dictionaries for a definition of the word "overwhelming". We have been transported to the realm of Lewis Carroll, wherein Humpty Dumpty declares "When I use a word it means just what I choose it to mean—neither more nor less".

Thus to suit your own convenience a majority of eight in the House of Commons represents "overwhelming" support. As for the British people, since they have never been consulted, you apparently assume their silence to mean that they are overwhelmingly behind you, anxious to become embroiled in the European cosmopolis and sever the links between themselves and their kinsmen overseas. As far as it has been possible to ascertain, they want nothing of the sort, but that fact will cause you no headache. You are content with the overwhelming support given you by a majority of eight.

* * * *

You can claim, Heaven knows, that you laboured hard to get that majority. On the eve of the vote you made it known that if it went against entry into Europe you and your colleagues would resign, thereby precipitating a general election from which the Labour Party, cashing-in on the soaring unemployment figures (the result of your Government's inept handling of the situation arising from the strike of the coal-miners) would almost certainly emerge victorious. The only inference was that many Conservatives would lose their seats and that those whose seats were safe but who had aspirations for office would be disappointed.

Not content with this general threat, which in essence was a play upon the venality of such members as were biddable, there were a series of interviews with Conservative Anti-Marketeers conducted by you or your colleagues or your party whips (in some cases, I understand, by several of you). What transpired has naturally not been made public, but what may be inferred was succinctly stated by Mr. Enoch Powell when he asked: "Who would complain if the political rewards of good behaviour and punishments for bad behaviour were sedulously applied to the wobblers and the waverers?" He continued. "That is what promises and threats are for; and as hope and credulity spring eternal, there will always be a supply of the gullible who mistake a kindly word for a firm undertaking, or a frown for a sentence of political death."

That such trashy, buyable creatures should have the power of determining the destiny of a mighty nation must make you very happy, Edward Heath, in that the exploitation of their venality produced undeniable results. Of the 47 Tory Anti-Marketeers who went into the lobby against you in October, only fifteen had the guts and the integrity to do so again in February.

* * * *

The methods used to reduce the original number to a point which enabled you to win your "overwhelming" victory were vile. Not only were the known dissidents approached in person, but the Central Office sent its paid hacks into their constituencies to try to organise political blackmail against them. Mr. Powell speaks witheringly of the situation created when "the apparatus of patronage and the system of bribes and threats is exported from Westminster to the country to constrain M.P.s to vote against what they know to be the wishes and believe to be the interests of their electors".

You must have been well aware, Edward Heath, that these despicable tactics were being employed to whip up support for your side, and you alone must bear the blame for the infamy. Most damnable of all was the threat to Ulster M.P.s and their constituents that if the party-line was not toed about entry into Europe, the British Government would withdraw its support from the Unionist cause in Northern Ireland. While the other measures were deeply dishonourable, this attempt at coercion on a matter of communal life and death was an act of political criminality of the worst kind—and you, Edward Heath, will go down in history as the worst kind of political criminal and the most effective traitor to your country to have disgraced its annals.

One fact must surely have occurred to even the most dim-witted of your followers. The titanic pressures which have been brought to bear on Parliamentarians and their constituents, your own ruthless bulldozing of the nation without the least regard to common decency, your breakneck speed to plunge Great Britain into the European Economic Community long before its thousands of implications could be read, let alone understood, the sheer irresponsibility and blatancy of your lying—all these things proclaim, not just your personal enthusiasm for a cause but the carrying out of a design which the international banking and general business interests consider to be cardinal to their plan, incubated through many years, of building a political, financial, commercial and strategic One World monopoly of power.

* * * *

Your own motivation is unknown to me. It cannot be supposed that the £36,000 prize awarded you by the FVS Foundation (created by the allegedly anti-Communist Herr Toepfer) and the additional £4,000 thrown in by some organisation in America were tied up in any way with your unprecedented fervour. When Mr. Harold Wilson (*The Times*, January 25) referred to you in the House of Commons as being "three times winner of the £38,000 prize for integrity from the Rotterness, Hartwell, Rees-Mogg foundation" I had no knowledge of any such set-up or of the awards made to you but it does occur to me that there is a cash nexus between you and the supranational cause you serve.

One thing, however, must be apparent to both of us. The bestowal upon you of large sums of money is an unquestionable indication of the quite abnormal importance attached to your labours by persons with power of patronage and with an unconcealed interest in supranational controls.

* * * *

Apart from your impenetrable hide and your ruthless determination to push through issues without regard to the people's wishes or to any accepted principle, you are not a man of distinction: people do not discern in you any great percipience or other outstanding mental quality. You have been chosen to do a hatchet-job on Britain for no reason except your total lack of scruple. It is all the more ironical that our thousand years of freedom so faithfully guarded by the sea and the stout hearts of our forbears should be brought to an inglorious end through the agency of so very mediocre a person as yourself.

Though all the foundations in the world load honours upon you in its name, the fact remains, Edward Heath, that you are not a man of integrity. Your resort to falsehood and political blackmail of the most contemptible kind casts derision on that title. If you succeed in handing over this historic Realm to foreign control, which is what membership of the E.E.C. means, we shall regard you as the French regarded Laval—as the agent of the enemy in overall possession.

In that event we shall become the Free British and fight you with all the lawful means at our disposal until we die. Never shall we allow it to be said that in the hour of treason there were no Britons to keep faith with the past or hand down a torch to the future.

Yours faithfully,

A. K. Chesterton

VIII

HOLD HIGH THE TORCH

By A. K. CHESTERTON

Candour # 521, April 1972.

THERE are critical times in the history of a nation—and today Great Britain faces the most menacing crisis in all her annals—when the poets should be heard. They illumine that which the party politicians have neither the sensitivity nor the will to express—the profoundest feelings of a people. More inspiring than all the oratory in Parliament was Rupert Brooke's greeting to the challenge of 1914—

> *"Honour has come back, as a king, to earth,*
>
> *And paid his subjects with a royal wage . . ."*

He did not live to see its dethronement just over four years later.

Lawrence Binyon wrote of our warrior dead the well-known lines—

> *"They shall not grow old, as we who are left grow old:*
>
> *Age shall not weary them, nor the years condemn.*
>
> *At the going down of the sun and in the morning*
>
> *We will remember them."*

On behalf of the dead, whom he was so soon to join, John McCrae pleaded with the living in lines no less famous—

> *"To you from failing hands we throw*

The Torch. Be yours to hold it high.

If you break faith with us who die

We shall not sleep, though poppies grow

In Flanders fields".

How well has faith been kept? How well is it being kept today? Most royally was it kept between the years 1939-45, when Honour again bestrode the land to command the same high purpose, the same nobility, the same heroic sacrifice to ensure an abiding British future.

* * * *

But since then, where to look for it? In what hearts?

While Geoffrey Rippon was negotiating for our national annihilation, did he on waking in the morning, or at sunset before dressing for his champagne dinners, pause even for a moment to think of all those mass graveyards so very near the scene? His face suggests that dedicated idealism is not one of his more notable characteristics. When Heath flew to his finest hour in Brussels, did he picture to himself those poppies far below, and think upon the hundreds of thousands of Britons — among them the betrayed Australians, Canadians, New Zealanders, South Africans, Rhodesians —who died that the British world should remain inviolate? Did he conceive of himself as their torchbearer, and, if so, was the torch he held aloft for Britain —or for Cosmopolis?

Those of us who are left have grown old, and the years have indeed condemned us, in a harsher sense than Binyon could have foreseen. We have been condemned by the years to witness, step by step, the betrayal of our country and of our fallen comrades as the political puppets who nominally rule us dance to the Wall Street tune, posturing their little hour to bring us along the path to the abyss. At this instant of time we are hovering upon its very edge.

The seeds of the betrayal may be as old as man, but in our own time we need trace them back no further than to the year 1917, when Rufus Isaacs, British Ambassador in Washington, arranged for a huge "American" loan to be repaid on call and in gold—a sufficiency of which we did not possess to cover the obligation. Since that disastrous event the moneylenders have had their grip on Britain's neck—a hold which only once, at Ottawa, was she able fleetingly to loosen. It is that grip which today takes us into Europe and tomorrow into the tyranny of One World.

* * * *

Not that all the exploiters of that earlier time were on the far side of the Atlantic. While the nation's youth was perishing on the Western Front, at home the war-profiteers were rubbing fat hands with glee as their fortunes soared. The moment the guns were silent they became as vultures, "noiselessly happy, feeding on the dead".

The inter-war years witnessed one capitalist ramp after another. Those who had lent to the Government when money was cheap demanded to be repaid after money had been made dear, for which purpose Winston Churchill had the folly (as he later admitted) to bring back the gold standard—a blow which hit the British workers straight between the eyes. As a result of this catastrophe, as of the even vaster catastrophe of the Great Slump and the ensuing depression (which placed the money-lenders well on the way to buying up pretty well the whole earth), almost an entire, generation of Britons stood at street corners begging for work which never came their way.

It was no wonder that trade unionists, as they watched the forces of Capitalism ravaging the world, should have taken a militant stance. Even though their earlier idealism long since gave way to a challenge in kind—materialism versus materialism—they were but emulating the reckless amok-runs of the other side.

Deplorably damaging and irresponsible as was the recent miners' strike; which hurt the poor much more than the rich, which inflicted much greater misery upon the aged and ailing than on the robust, and which threatened the whole nation with extinction—dreadful as that factional war against the community must be accounted, it was not one-hundredth part as wickedly self-seeking as is the Capitalist drive to possess the earth which the Heath-Rippon gang are going all-out to hasten. Time and again have these hacks proclaimed the need to build up ever bigger international corporations, which are already being turned into giant monopolies in the Common Market countries. What the Big Boys behind the scenes are grabbing is not £20 a week, but the entire human inheritance.

* * * *

In as far as the British share of the inheritance is endangered by any faction, be it Capital or Labour, that faction breaks faith with the men who died. So great and almost all-embracing is the betrayal that only a few of us attempt—as we have done through all the weary years—to hold high the torch thrown to us by our fallen comrades who willed that there should be a British future. All the money and all the power in the world are ranged against us, as indeed is all the ignorance, all the sloth, all the disdain. We have as weapons only words, but we must see to it that those words have the impact of bullets.

The all-too-nice are horrified to find such a thing as treason given its proper name. Some dear friends of mine overseas handed two English visitors the *Candour* booklet *Common Market Suicide* to read. After a page or two they flung it aside in disgust, affirming that they were prepared to consider facts but not invective. The booklet is crammed with facts, especially concerning Wall Street's involvement in the plot, but because treason was called treason they recoiled aghast.

* * * *

It would be useless, of course, to tell such people that the present war between Truth and Falsehood is more important than any fought with sword or lance or fire-arm. Yet such it is. I find a certain wry amusement in wondering whether those Englishmen (assuming them to be male, because I did not ask) had ever taken part in a bayonet-charge, and if so whether in the final dash their faces registered the same supercilious air of disdain.

Our call is not to such as these. It is to real men and real women who place country above party and will continue to do so even in the face of doom. The few have been known to succeed where the many have failed. Honour may again return as a king and that shall be the only wage we seek. It will not happen unless we keep the torch alight, to make all men aware that our comrades died for some nobler purpose than the creation of a paradise for monopolists and racketeers.

IX

APPEAL TO THE QUEEN

By A. K. CHESTERTON

Candour # 523, June 1972.

MAY it please Your Majesty,

Several times during the last two decades I have ventured to exercise the right of British subjects to petition their Monarch, not on my own behalf but on behalf of loyalists at home and overseas with good reason to believe that successive British Governments were betraying them. On every such occasion I received an acknowledgment from Your Majesty's private secretary informing me that at your command the petition had been sent to the Ministry concerned, which advised that no action be taken—not surprisingly as it was always a Ministry against which the complaint had been made. Your Majesty will readily understand that the procedure raised in our minds the question as to whether the right of petition to the Throne still possesses validity, or whether it should be written off as an anachronism.

The question today assumes more importance than ever before during the last thousand years. The issue at stake arises from the determination of Your Majesty's Government to ensure that the Queen-in-Parliament is no longer supreme in this ancient land, but becomes progressively subordinated to an alien authority established on foreign soil.

It is understandable that Your Majesty in the ordinary course should be reliant on the advice of your Ministers, but with submission the present situation is not ordinary and can only be met by the exercise of the residual powers invested in the Crown. What makes this submission the more cogent is that, as the Ministers have not scrupled to mislead Parliament and the nation, the strong probability is that the advice tendered Your Majesty has also been trimmed to further their own internationalist designs.

Your Majesty's First Minister, for example, has assured Parliament that the adherence of Your Majesty's Realm to the European Economic Community will not entail the erosion of essential national sovereignty. The Right Honourable gentleman did not define the word "essential", but if Your Majesty should wish the matter to be put to the test, the evidence is available in the Treaty of Rome, the provisions of which cover all the departments of life wherein sovereignty has meaning. Instead of taking its clauses one by one, therefore, I would refer Your Majesty to a passage from a book by one of your former Ministers, Mr. Douglas Jay, which provides a complete answer to Mr. Heath.

I quote: "A decision by the E.E.C. Commission automatically becomes legally binding and enforceable in the courts of the member-countries without those countries' Governments or Parliaments ever having been consulted—or normally having the power to challenge the decision after the event. This is also true of its directives, regulations and, in a negative sense, authorisations. On many subjects the Commission can make such decisions, without even the Council of Ministers of the E.E.C. being consulted, or in some cases having the right to reverse or amend a decision afterwards. These subjects, on which the Commission has sovereign power of legislation without responsibility to anyone, include the application of the rules of free competition to nationalised industries or to any industries enjoying special or exclusive rights or to monopoly services; the crucial right of a Government to enforce measures to defend its currency for more than a short period; the grant of state aid in many forms to industry; and so forth. On all these issues the Commission, without consulting any Ministers or elected persons at all, can order member-Governments to do what the Commission chooses; and their orders automatically become enforceable in the 'municipal' courts of the member-countries—in plain English, Britain, if we were rash enough to sign the Rome Treaty." If these factors alone—even apart from specific clauses written into the Treaty of Rome—are held by Mr. Heath not to amount to an erosion of essential sovereignty, then I would respectfully suggest to Your Majesty the need for setting up a Royal Enquiry to investigate the abuse of semantics in the furtherance of dangerous Governmental policies.

Such an Enquiry would embrace the terminology not only of Your Majesty's First Minister but also that of the Lord Chancellor, whose position in the legal hierarchy should surely impose on him a special responsibility for the right use of words. How far he is from recognising such obligation may be judged from this report in *The Times*: 'Entry into the E.E.C. would not diminish the sovereignty of the British Parliament, Lord Hailsham of St. Marylebone, Lord Chancellor, said in London last night. He said at the Grotius Dinner of the British Institute of International and Comparative Law that the European Community introduced a new concept into the fabric of law not because it abridged the concept of sovereignty, which in his judgment it did not, but because, unlike other treaty obligations, it introduced a new source of law directly applicable in the municipal jurisdictions of the member states. The conceptions introduced by the Rome treaty were not destructive of sovereignty and would not become so unless individual members sought to enforce the terms of the treaty or the decrees of the European Court, by force of arms."

This must seem to Your Majesty, as it does to many of your subjects, a gross misuse of words designed as a piece of special (and specious) pleading to confuse and mislead the nation. It is difficult to decide which of the two propositions argued by Lord Hailsham is the more astounding. That E.E.C. enactments, as soon as the Treaty of Rome is signed, will have immediate force of law in Your Majesty's Realm is common knowledge, and the Lord Chancellor's argument—that this is no more than a new concept introduced into the fabric of law which does not abridge the concept of sovereignty —can only be described as chop-logic amounting to intellectual dishonesty.

Lord Hailsham's second proposition, that sovereignty can only be abridged by armed intervention, is fantastic. It declares, in effect, that law is not law until its observance is enforced. What the Noble Lord may have had in mind is the saying—I think by Anatole France —that a judge without policemen would be an idle dreamer. Odious though the Treaty of Rome undoubtedly is, it cannot cause Your Majesty or your subjects any pleasure to think that Your Majesty's Government contemplates entering Europe in the cynical belief that only a war would have power to force it to honour the obligations it has undertaken.

Moreover, I would submit for Your Majesty's consideration the view that Lord Hailsham is mistaken in supposing that the terms of the Treaty or the decrees of the European Court could only be enforced by military sanctions. Your Majesty's judges could be called upon by Community members to hear complaints of breaches of E.E.C. law or the non-fulfilment of other contractual obligations, and if Parliament attempted to bar access to them, the other members of the Community could—and no doubt would—call for economic sanctions, to which our economic integration will make us all too vulnerable. Our financial assets placed under E.E.C. control, or in keeping of member states, would almost certainly be frozen, and having become progressively dissociated from our overseas markets and spheres of influence we would find ourselves alone in a harsh and unforgiving world.

Therefore, Your Majesty, your petitioner, writing on behalf of very many of your other loyal subjects, pleads with you to use the residual powers constitutionally vested in the Crown not to give the Royal Assent to any Parliamentary enactment that would annul or diminish the rights of the Monarch and peoples of Britain to be masters in their own land. Were Your Majesty to accede to this plea you would be acting in accordance with the time-honoured tradition whereby the peoples have been accorded the protection of their Monarch against the tyranny of those who would oppress them or otherwise betray their interests. The power of the barons in the Middle Ages is now wielded by a vast complex of financial, industrial and commercial consortia seeking to become international monopolies, and it is on their behalf, and not on behalf of Your Majesty and the people of Britain, that the Government devils. This truth was implicit in a statement of one of Your Majesty's Ministers that today the international corporation has more to offer mankind than the nation state, which must be taken to mean that our country would fare better under the aegis of the international financial power-masters of New York and London than under Your Majesty's rule. The Ministerial statement, lacking nothing in blatancy, in almost any other age would have been construed as treasonable and as such would it have been treated.

We seek Your Majesty's protection against the international enemy's fifth column now entrenched in Parliament, Pulpit and Press, and in so doing I quote some noble words from a speech made twenty-five years ago:

"Let us say with Rupert Brooke 'Now, God be thanked Who has matched us with His hour.' . . . Most of you have read in the history books the proud saying of William Pitt that England had saved herself by her exertions and would save Europe by her example. But in our time we may say that the British Empire has saved the world first and has now to save itself after the battle is won. I think that is an even

finer thing than was done in the days of Pitt, and it is for us who have grown up in these years of danger and glory to see that it is accomplished in the long years of peace that we all hope stretch ahead. If we all go forward together with an unwavering faith, a high courage and a quiet heart, we shall be able to make of this ancient Commonwealth which we all love so dearly an even grander thing— more free, more prosperous, more happy and more powerful influence for good in the world—than it has been in the greatest days of our forefathers. To accomplish that we must give nothing less than the whole of ourselves. There is a motto which has been borne by many of my ancestors—a noble motto, 'I serve'. Those words were an inspiration to many bygone heirs to the Throne when they made their knightly dedication as they came to manhood. I cannot do quite as they did, but through the inventions of science I can do what was not possible for any of them. I can make my solemn act of dedication with a whole Empire listening. I should like to make that dedication now. It is very simple. I declare before you all that my whole life, whether it be long or short, shall be devoted to your service and the service of our great Imperial Family to which we all belong but I shall not have strength to carry out this resolution alone unless you join in it with me, as I now invite you to do. I know that your support will be unfailingly given. God help me to make good my vow, and God bless all of you who are willing to share in it."

Your Majesty, millions throughout the British world were willing to share in the vow you made when broadcasting that speech at Cape Town on your twenty-first birthday. Many still wish to share in it. Many are still prepared to give the whole of themselves. But many others, through force of circumstances, have dropped by the wayside. Loyal subjects who built up civilisation in Kenya and elsewhere in East Africa, and who have been betrayed by successive British Governments, now live in other lands and the words they speak are bitter. Others, more impressively, remain silent: they turn their heads away and look sadly into the distance. So with the staunch-hearted Rhodesians against whom Your Majesty's Governments for seven years have been waging economic war. The very word "British", once so proudly claimed, now has evil connotations for them. So with the South Africans, forced out of the Commonwealth by the insults of pseudo-sophisticates and parvenus newly emerged from the bush. Now comes the turn of the Australians, the Canadians and New Zealanders—the warriors who supplied storm-troops second to none in the service of Your Majesty's royal father and royal grandfather. What are they to think when their goods must jump tariff walls to reach their traditional British markets while goods from Germany, France, Italy, Turkey and all the other E.E.C. members or affiliates pour in duty-free? What is their response when they themselves are treated as aliens in the land for which they gave so much?

Finally, there are Your Majesty's subjects in the United Kingdom, who witness with near despair the drive by the British Government to hand over their power of sovereign decision to a cosmopolitan cabal, and who know that, after the Third Reading, the Bill now before Parliament will require only one more process to become the law of the land. That process is vital —the securing of the Royal Assent. We plead with Your Majesty to withhold Assent until such time as the wish of your subjects as a whole—as distinct from that of Parliamentary careerists and ideologues—can be made known.

Your Majesty's subjects do not doubt for a moment that you have faithfully kept your vow of dedication made at Cape Town twenty-five years ago. They have watched with pride and pleasure your gracious bearing on overseas tours, and at ceremonies at home which demanded, and invariably received, the cheerful endurance of long-sustained exertion and tedium. Within the compass of what Your Majesty has considered your Monarchical role not one of your subjects fails to agree that the Royal motto "I serve" has been most royally upheld.

Their one great worry, however, is lest the scope of the Monarchy has become accepted as being confined to ceremonial duties and formalities the performance of which Ministers of the Crown may take for granted. If this be indeed the case, the tradition of constitutional checks and balances must be regarded as having been thrown into the discard, so that the people are without hope of effective final resort to their Sovereign for protection. In such an event the Queen-in-Parliament is a misnomer, because then the Queen is no longer sovereign and next year Parliament will lose its own sovereignty.

Your Majesty will perhaps permit me to point out, which I do with the very greatest respect, that the residual powers vested in the Crown, if no longer exercised, have not been filched by Act of Parliament but voluntarily allowed to lapse. They could be re-asserted. What deeply troubles us is the thought that there may no longer be the will or even the desire to use those powers. Substance was given to our fear when H.R.H. Prince Charles, soon after his investiture as Prince of Wales, said in an interview recorded on B.B.C. television that he knew he was required to do a "stooge's job" and had no objection to being a "stooge". Your Majesty, the British people do not relish the thought of their Sovereign or the Heir to the Throne filling so ignoble a role, which must mean in effect being the puppet of Edward Heath or Harold Wilson, who are themselves often mere servitors of others whose identity is seldom disclosed.

Your Majesty will remember the inspiring words of Queen Elizabeth the First who deemed it "foul shame" that foreigners should seek to invade her Realm. What kind of shame would she have deemed it had Burghley and Walsingham been discovered following a policy designed to give away the Realm to a Continental hotchpotch? What would have happened to them cannot be doubted. Times, we know, have changed and it is unfortunately not possible for Heath to be sent to the Tower. Unless I am mistaken, however, it is within the power of Your Majesty to give your peoples a lead in defeating his machinations and thereby help to ensure for Great Britain a great future as a sovereign independent Power.

Should Your Majesty give this lead there would undoubtedly follow what is called "a grave constitutional crisis", but it would be only a small matter relative to the "gloom of earthquake and eclipse" that must ensue when we are overtaken by the catastrophe of adherence to the European Economic Community.

Millions of Your Majesty's subjects would be overjoyed to range behind you in proud support and generations of Britons still to come would thank God for a Queen whose quality had been equal to the greatest challenge in the history of their beloved country.

I remain Your Majesty's liegeman,

A. K. CHESTERTON

X
STAND FAST!

By A. K. CHESTERTON

Candour # 524, July 1972.

DESPITE the error in The Times (which it failed to correct next day) in reporting that the Clause moved by Sir Elwyn Jones calling for the supremacy of Parliament in all E.E.C. matters had been passed, the European Communities Bill went through the Committee stage of the House of Commons unamended.

To secure its miserable majority of 13 the Government again resorted to the most blatant argument for dishonesty ever heard in Westminster. It was, in effect, what the ineffable Lord Chancellor had put forward when he asserted that the E.E.C. could only force Great Britain to honour her undertaking by making war.

The Solicitor-General said it had been suggested that if Britain withdrew from the treaties they would face incalculable claims for damages. He asked "Who would enforce them, and how?" Sir Geoffrey Howe then made a statement which indicates that the Government is not only cynically dishonest, but living in a verbal cloud-cuckoo-land wherein even the most lunatic proposition may pass unchallenged. I quote *The Times* report:

"The heart of the matter was how to reconcile the irreconcilable—the supremacy of Community law with the sovereignty of Parliament. These were the two factors the country had to balance. It was a task

which would have had to be undertaken by any Government who succeeded in negotiating a settlement."

* * * *

There is no reason to suppose that Sir Geoffrey is off his head, but in truth nobody but a madman would attempt to reconcile that which in his own words is "irreconcilable". All that the Solicitor-General's Mad-Hattery amounts to is that the Government, with a miniscule majority, has ceded British sovereign rights to E.E.C. law. The general level of intelligence among his hearers is such that he feels forced to soften the harsh fact by a semantic juggling act which has no basis in reality and so conceals the fact that Britain's sovereignty faces doom.

Now is indeed the darkest hour. Up and down the country more and more Anti-Market organisations have sprung into being to fight the menace. Once the Bill becomes an Act, so-called "realists' will be tempted to regard the situation as hopeless. We urge them to resist the temptation. We beg them to remain in the thick of the battle. We say, what we have said over and over again, that battles apparently lost can be won. Miracles do happen when there is the strength of character

.... *"to hope, till Hope creates*

From its own wreck the thing it contemplates;

Neither to change, nor falter, nor repent;

This, like thy glory, Titan, is to be

Good, great and free;

This is alone Life, Joy, Empire and Victory."

What is *Candour* that it should be so bold as to send forth this Promethean challenge? The question can be answered. *Candour* was the first, and for some years the only, journal to fight the Common

Market menace. From the very start of Macmillan's initial campaign to negotiate with the "Six" a European free trade area with a common tariff system which would by-pass the Treaty of Rome, we asserted that any such move must entail the abandonment of our complementary economy overseas in favour of entering a competitive system. As others were alerted to the economic dangers, we laid increasing emphasis on sovereignty and—whether or not cause and effect who can say?— in course of time our very language was heard on other lips and can often be read almost word for word in Hansard.

At any rate it can be established that *Candour* first raised the standard of revolt against an Establishment determined to commit national hari-kari, that we have persisted in our stand against tremendous odds and that one remark alone has fully justified our entire case—that of Minister of Trade Davies, who said that the international corporation had more to offer mankind than the nation state. In a single sentence Mono-poly Capitalism was revealed as the motivating influence driving craven Governments into the all-pervasive corruption of cosmopolitan Europe.

Those are the grounds which we believe entitle us, without presumption, to call on all true and perceptive patriots not to abandon their country's cause at the hour when most their help is needed. At the year's beginning we declared that we would make an all-out effort to save our national sovereignty and we are trying to fulfil that undertaking. Much of our literature has been republished for mass distribution, which we supply at sub-economic cost and free to those who cannot afford to pay.

Many other organisations are now engaged in the same work. All want volunteers who will help to distribute their publications. All are in need of funds. Those patriots who do not like *Candour* methods — particularly our insistence on giving treason its proper name—will today find many admirable bodies working by other means to the same end. We ask them to support these organisations to the utmost of their power. In the same way we urge those who find useful such articles as *Hold High The Torch, Open Letter to Edward Heath, and Appeal to The Queen* to back *Candour* by personal and financial aid. The need and the hour are alike critical.

If we are dragged into the Common Market, let our protest be a massive one, so that when legislative, administrative and economic disasters knock us down next year there will be a resistance movement in being strong enough to put Britain on its feet again as a sovereign nation with its own great and distinctive part to play in the shaping of the future.

XI

WE MUST GET OUT

By A. K. CHESTERTON

Candour # 527, November 1972.

EDWARD HEATH is cock-a-hoop. Having successfully secured for the Economic Communities Bill a marginal passage through the House of Commons, its acceptance by a large majority of the House of Lords, and the granting of the Royal Assent, the Prime Minister now treads the earth with the air of a man of destiny. During the debate which followed all these processes he was described by the Parliamentary correspondent of *The Times* as having "contemptuously swept aside, as though swatting bluebottles" the arguments of his critics. "This time Britain is there" (in the Common Market) has become his triumphant note.

It was a dismal fact which could scarcely be disputed. When Heath went to Brussels in February (the notable occasion when a woman on quite other grounds smothered him with ink) the most we imagined his intention to be was to sign a declaration of intent, whereas his recent utterances would suggest that he signed the lethal Treaty of Rome, or if not that a treaty firmly committing us to obey its requirements past, present and to come, which would amount to much the same thing.

* * * *

Thereafter, having received constitutional support for a completely unconstitutional measure—in other words, constitutional approval of a vile act of treason against the British people at home and abroad—all he had to do in any subsequent Debate was to tell his opponents that what they opposed was in fact a *fait-accompli*.

It so happens, however, that there are some millions of us in Great Britain and scattered across the world, who refuse, and will always refuse, to accept the belief that what our forefathers so stalwartly defended throughout the centuries and for which in our own century the youth of the nation has shed so much blood, is a bauble to be disposed of by anybody, let alone a coterie of unmeritable men such as Edward Heath, Geoffrey Rippon and their like. National sovereignty, the right to be masters in our home, is of such spiritual and practical value to us that its abandonment not only mocks the high endeavour of times past but brings our history as a proud and independent nation to an obscene end.

* * * *

How have those elected to represent us been beguiled into giving their consent to this enormous and deadly treason? Mostly, it must be said, by sheer lying. Edward Heath at the outset declared that adherence to the Treaty of Rome would entail no abandonment of essential national sovereignty, a statement which the clauses of the Treaty themselves refuted. Then came the turn of Lord Hailsham, the irresponsible playboy of British politics who never finds difficulty in obtaining high Cabinet rank, to go one better and say that E.E.C. membership, so far from lessening national sovereignty, would greatly increase it. The same argument, more soberly stated, was used by Heath in the Commons Debate of October 23.

Asked by the Opposition about what assurances there were that monies would be made available by the Community for regional development in Britain, the Prime Minister could only reply that the principle of providing such resources had been fully accepted by the E.E.C., and added, as though to clinch the argument, that Britain would be represented on the Council of Ministers "with full powers to decide matters". His half-baked followers in the House cheered this statement as though it was pregnant of meaning, whereas in truth it meant nothing.

* * * *

Norway, having very sensibly refused to join the Common Market, the Council of Ministers will number nine, of whom one will be British. In what possible way can it be said that the British representative will have "full powers" to decide any matter, let alone the amount of the Community budget to be allocated to regional development in the British Isles? If five Ministers of the Council were to gang up against him, as assuredly time after time they will, the British Minister would find himself totally devoid of power to influence the expenditure of a single pfennig, centime or new penny.

Heath's assurance was thus not only misleading but infantile. What manner of men are they in Parliament who not only accept such pronouncements as making good sense but, without further consideration, give away a Kingdom—in fact several Kingdoms—on the strength of them? Although there are a few whose intellectual ability is outstanding, most members are at best mediocre and at the worse "plain dumb", but the sinister thing is that whether they be highly intelligent or verging on stupidity, they all tend (with very few exceptions) to unite behind even the most preposterous Party policy, completely without regard to the national interest, which they take as a matter of course to be identical with whatever it is that is being propounded. There can be no better example of this amoral approach to matters of the profoundest consequence than the acceptance of Heath's assurance that regional development in Britain will be safeguarded by the presence on the Council of Ministers of a British

Minister with "full power to decide matters", the fact that he can be outvoted eight to one apparently notwithstanding.

* * * *

Professionalism alone can account for such abject abandonment of the British people's most cherished values. Apart from the lucrative sidelines usually open to biddable M.P.'s, the fact that they earn their living from their Parliamentary salaries gives them a vested interest in retaining seats that could be endangered were they to incur the displeasure of their Party leadership. The threat can be made a general one, as when Bulldozer Heath, determined to push through the E.E.C. Bill, said that in the event of failure the Government would resign. That would place in hazard all those occupying Ministerial office, check the ambition of aspirants to such posts, almost certainly unseat Members in marginal constituencies, and cause particular trouble from Central Office in the constituencies of noted rebels. Indeed, as Mr. Enoch Powell pointed out, Central Office had already begun to put pressure on certain constituency organisations wherein Members were disposed to vote against the Government and save the country from being plunged into the European vortex. The only way the British people can counter political professionalism and political blackmail of the kind described is to make clear that their displeasure is more to be feared than anything Party H.Q. can do—after all, it is upon their franchise that Members depend for election. Nobody supposes that this demonstration is an easy job to perform, but it can be done.

The House of Lords, of course, has run to seed through several decades. Those who belong to it by right of birth have become so mixed-up with the plutocracy that there is no longer any sense of *noblesse oblige*. Most of them are a bad joke. As for Life Peers, the less said about them the better. There is no wonder that the E.E.C.

Bill, given quite a rough passage through the House of Commons, should have bounced in and out of the House of Lords with supersonic speed.

* * * *

There then remained only one more process before the Bill became law—the granting of the Royal Assent.

Hundreds of thousands (perhaps millions) of Her Majesty's loyal subjects hastened to petition the Queen not to relinquish her own sovereignty and that of her Realms by granting her Assent. We were all told that our petitions had been sent to the Prime Minister, and when we gently remonstrated with Court officials by pointing out that our pleas had been to our Sovereign Liege and not to Edward Heath, their reply was that the action taken accorded with constitutional custom. The word 'constitutional' in this context seemed to some of us strange. Is Royal Approval now another term for Prime Ministerial Approval and if so should that fact not be made known?

One staunch fighter in the battle for national survival, not at all content with the official rejoinder, put before the Queen's Private Secretary a blunt request to know whether her letter had been read by Her Majesty before being sent to No. 10. The reply came that the Queen reads all the letters and petitions sent to her. It would be indelicate to question information from so high a source, but as the letters and petitions received each week, covering a vast range of subjects, must amount to thousands, one can but wonder at Her Majesty's stamina.

* * * *

Assuming that the official's assurance is to be taken as its face-value, and not as a traditional fiction, one thing becomes certain—the Queen must know the case against her Realm being taken over by a foreign cabal as well as, if not better than, the case for the pro-Marketeers. It may even be that Her Majesty regards the E.E.C. proposals with the profoundest suspicion but considers none the less that the withholding of sanction against the advice of her Ministerial advisers would be contrary to custom and lead to a constitutional crisis of the first magnitude. Only a Monarch of very great strength of mind and clarity of vision would undertake so momentous a step, and it would be unreasonable to blame Her Majesty should she not possess these qualities.

However, at this point there is one further consideration of the utmost importance which it would be folly to ignore. Her Majesty is not only Queen of the United Kingdom: she is also the Queen of Australia, the Queen of New Zealand and the Queen of Canada. Did she, assuming that her's was the power to grant or deny the Royal Assent, consult not only her Ministerial advisers in Great Britain, but also her Ministerial advisers in her Realms overseas? If so, Her Majesty must have been aware of a sharp clash of opinion between the latter and the former and that entry into the Common Market would have the result of still further alienating her subjects overseas. Whether the Queen deliberately made a choice between these two options we shall never know, but what we cannot fail to know is that through the action of the British Government the loyalties of our kinsmen who have sacrificed so much for the British cause may well be weakened to vanishing point. For what purpose?

* * * *

Part of the answer was given by the former Chief Executive of Rothschild Freres, President Pompidou, on October 19, when he said that within a decade the E.E.C. must be turned into European union and Prime Minister Heath apparently agreed. This step, long foretold by *Candour*, will be part of the process of subjecting mankind to a World Government tyranny. Whatever residual powers are left to us after we join the Common Market on January 1 will be swept away, and with them our cherished Monarchy.

The mere fact of our adhering to the E.E.C. will enable One-Wonders to get busy stealthily undermining the institutions upon which we set great store, but even if no such objective as European union had been decreed, it would still be necessary for us to seize the first opportunity to get out of the European Economic community and regain masterdom over our own destiny. Although unconquered since 1066, the fifth columnism of the Heath-Rippon cabal ensures that on January 1 we shall undergo a period of being placed under alien rule.

It is a matter of honour for every Briton worthy of the name lawfully to resist subjection to the conquerors rule and work without ceasing to get us out of the foreign cesspool.

XII

CONFOUND THEIR POLITICS

By A. K. CHESTERTON

Candour # 528, December 1972.

WHEN Britons sing the lines of the National Anthem which relate to the Queen's enemies, beseeching God to

"Confound their politics

Frustrate their knavish tricks"

they visualise foreign powers envious of her Realms and anxious to seize and despoil them. Not for an instant do they visualise those enemies as being within the gate, fifth columnists occupying the highest posts in the land and charged with the responsibility of tendering advice to the Monarch.

Yet today these are the men, up to their eyes in treason which has become "legal", whose policies and knavish tricks should and must be confounded; these are the traitors who conspire with a foreign cabal to rob the Queen and her subjects of their sovereignty. But while millions of Her Majesty's subjects have protested, the Queen-because of the execrable advice tendered her-has bestowed the Royal cachet on the conspiracy, thereby bringing us to the verge of national extinction.

As the Bill to subordinate this Kingdom to a cosmopolitan "elite" of financial and commercial monopolists was passing through Parliament, Buckingham Palace became swamped with letters and petitions begging the Queen to withhold the Royal Assent but these were all sent on the instant to No. 10 Downing Street. A Court official, in reply to a direct question, affirmed that Her Majesty read all the letters addressed to her-a statement which I, for one, frankly disbelieve. Even so, it is not credible that the Palace is so insulated from the outside world that the Queen was unaware of the huge body of dissent within her Realm or that a vital clause in the Bill scraped through the House of Commons by a majority of five. Why, then, was no notice taken of the passionate protests of all Her Majesty's most loyal subjects? Why did the Queen, instead of making use of her residual powers, allow this shocking Bill to become law?

The reason easiest to argue is that Her Majesty, remembering that she is a Constitutional Monarch, feels obliged to put the Royal seal on whatever enactment the Government is able to induce Parliament to pass. This makes good enough sense if we assume that the Monarch's residual powers have in fact become extinct, that the British people can no longer look to their Sovereign for ultimate protection, that the Sovereign through long disuse of the Royal veto is powerless to protect them. If such be the truth of the matter, it would surely be more honest for the minds of Britons to be disabused and for the securing of the Royal Assent to be dropped as a piece of useless and misleading ritual.

Should Her Majesty have considered that she had no alternative other than to allow the E.E.C. Bill to become law, her reasoning could have been understood, But the unscrupulous men tendering her advice were not content with that one act: nothing would satisfy them short of bringing the Queen into the arena as a partisan on their side. The giving or withholding of the Royal Assent can be regarded as an Act of State, but outside that context to express an opinion on so vital an issue would be to enter the field of political argument, where one would not expect to encounter one's Sovereign, and where Her Majesty would never have gone but for the guiding hands of her traitorous Ministers.

I quote what happened on such an occasion from the *Daily Telegraph*:

"The Queen last night effectively scotched the notion which some anti-marketeers have assiduously peddled: that she ought to be averse to Britain's entry into the Common Market because of the alleged loss of sovereignty entailed. In a speech at the state banquet she gave at Windsor Castle for the Federal German President and Frau Heinemann, she showed herself an enthusiastic pro-marketeer. So far, she said, the unity of Europe had lain beyond the far horizon. But now the nine countries of the enlarged community had set it as a goal 'within our reach'. Already the Community had created the largest trading unit in the world, and one of the most powerful economic groupings. It was a great achievement".

It is, with all respect, grossly unfair both to Her Majesty and to those of her subjects who place the greatest value upon their national heritage to set them on what would be a collision course were it not for the fact that the loyalists are too devoted to the institution of Monarchy to allow their dismay, indeed their near-despair, to turn them, for whatever reason, against the Ruling Monarch.

The only way out of the impasse is to recognise that the Ruling Monarch in reality no longer rules, that the Royal Assent for all practical purposes has become the Prime Ministerial Assent, and that when the Queen spoke at the Windsor State Banquet the form of the words which she uttered almost certainly did not originate in her own mind, but was composed by some functionary at No. 10 or perhaps at the Foreign Office. Therefore, when we say that the establishing of the European Economic Community is not a great achievement, that the adherence of our once splendid nation to this cosmopolitan midden is far and away the biggest disaster in British history, we are contradicting not the Queen but Edward Heath and the powers behind Heath who have manoeuvred him into the Premiership for this one all-important purpose.

How far Her Majesty has an understanding of the grave implications of the E.E.C. Act we have no means of knowing. Again and again and again during the last several years they have been pointed out to her in innumerable letters and petitions, and if Her Majesty's interest in international affairs is even half as extensive as is her knowledge of horses and horsemanship certain fundamental factors must surely have entered the forefront of her mind. One of the weightiest factors is that what the Queen's speech-writer called "a great achievement" involves nothing less than the literal alienation of her own subjects overseas. When the Treaty of Rome becomes the law of the land, every German, every Frenchman, every Belgian, every Dane and every Italian will have as much right to the usufruct of the United Kingdom as native Britons, whereas Australians, New Zealanders, Canadians, Rhodesians and others who came instantly to the help of the Mother Country in 1914 and 1939 will be foreigners, allowed to work here only by voucher based on a quota system. The mere thought of so preposterous an arrangement must bring sadness into the hearts of even the humblest of Her Majesty's subjects. It cannot, surely, leave the Queen herself unmoved.

One remembers the T.V. interview given by the present Prince of Wales when he said he knew the part assigned to him was a stooge's role and declared that he had no objection to being a stooge. If that is also Her Majesty's view of her own Royal duty—and where does one look for any counter-indications?— then the greater becomes the obligation of those of us who are not content that our country should come under foreign domination, or that our kinsmen overseas should become aliens among us, to do all in our power to defeat the Queen's enemies who use Her Majesty for their own ignoble purposes. The responsibility is not God's but our own to confound their politics and frustrate their knavish tricks, and if we go about the business with sufficient determination and courage the more likely we are to secure God's help.

After all these years of soldiering-on, God knows we need it.

XIII

EUROPE - THE TRUTH

By A. K. CHESTERTON

Candour # 530, February 1973.

FOR British people the world over, those at any rate aware of its significance, the yielding of the old year to the new was the saddest hour of their lives. It symbolised the passing away of their nationhood, the end of the British epoch—the most momentous, the most beneficent, the greatest epoch in world history. Eyes not easily moved to tears became misty. It was to cease upon the midnight, but assuredly not without pain—the hurt of more than a thousand years of high endeavour derided and thrown to the winds was unbearably poignant. To avoid so ignoble an end Britons throughout the centuries had fought and died; their womenfolk had sacrificed husbands, sons, sweethearts, brothers, with the sole consolation that in so doing they helped to make secure the British future. And what a mockery has now been made of that belief.

Whatever we may be able to recover from the wreckage, the British world as we have known it has been given its quietus: to pretend otherwise would be folly. Sovereignty has been surrendered, nominally to a cabal in Brussels, but actually to ruthless financial powers which 'fight by shuffling papers' and which hide their intentions beneath a mountain of deceptive policies and bogus ideals. These vested interests, which we shall scrutinise in a few moments, are under no obligation to the British people, and should they pounce upon us, as they have done, to suck the life-blood out of us, the fault lies in part with our own lack of awareness, but more particularly in the treacherous activities of the politicians whom we pay high salaries to maintain watch and ward over the nation and who have despicably betrayed their trust. The fact that these creatures have managed to carry with them a Monarch endowed with much graciousness but not with a grasp of world affairs fails to absolve them from the moral, if not the legal, responsibility of committing High Treason. If to make that statement and to name the traitors is to lay myself open to a charge of criminal libel, then it is a charge I am prepared to face.

The names are legion—their owners are to be found teeming in Westminster,␣Whitehall, Fleet Street, Broadcasting House, Lambeth and up and down the country—so I must be content with the mention of a few. Heading the Dishonours List are Heath, Home, Hailsham and Rippon. The four of them, acting on the stated principle that the multinational corporation has more to offer mankind than has the national state, took the lead in sacrificing the British nations at home and overseas upon the altar of cosmopolitan greed and power. In so doing they lied throughout, either deliberately or because the vitiating atmosphere of Parliament has rotted their brains.

Heath lied when he said that the Government would not take Great Britain into the European Common Market without the full-hearted consent of the British Parliament and people. He lied again when he assured the House of Commons that adherence to the E.E.C. involved no erosion of essential sovereignty. His whole campaign has been one long record of falsehood, of bringing duresse to bear on party dissidents and of using the taxpayers money for his own tendentious propaganda.

Home lied when he assured the citizens of the White Commonwealth that their status in Britain would not be inferior to that of European foreigners. Hailsham, whose gyrations between the Upper and Lower Houses resemble the antics of a monkey-on-the-stick, added to this orgy of falsity the startling assertion that, so far from British sovereignty being eroded, it would be greatly expanded. The argument appeared to be that although Britain's control over her own affairs would be reduced to one-ninth, her acquisition of one-ninth control over the affairs of other countries would more than compensate for the loss. It is a grim thought that we have as Lord Chancellor a man who expects so lunatic a proposition to be believed and even grimmer should he believe it himself.

The total absence of any sense of deeply dishonourable, let alone treasonable, conduct in the comments made in press and pulpit and on television is matched by the total lack of sensibility in recognising the enormous emotional upheaval in every party of the British world which the treachery has caused. Apart from journals such as *Candour* and *Spearhead*, one has to go as far as Washington D.C. to read any true appreciation of what British patriots feel. I quote from its *Evening Star* and *Daily News* which states in an article referring to New Zealanders:

"They are bothered, indeed. The umbilical cord to the mother country is about to be cut because of Britain's entry into the Common Market. Only with the greatest difficulty did New Zealand succeed in getting Common Market members to agree to let Britain temporarily continue to import 71 per cent of the butter which New Zealand has been sending to the United Kingdom. Britain still takes about half of New Zealand's $1.2 billion annual exports. As the mother country is drawn more tightly into Europe, what then? There is anger at the prospect of making New Zealanders aliens in Britain, and Britons aliens in New Zealand. Neither country wants it, but Britain's immigration policies must henceforth be co-ordinated with Western Europe. So New Zealanders who have a strong sentimental attachment to the old country, see a bleak day when Italians will be able to move to England more freely than they."

* * * *

This is not the only umbilical cord to be severed nor are the New Zealanders the only people to feel affronted in their innermost being. The sum total of broken cords, of loyalties spurned, of the agony of a great family of nations torn apart, meets with as fierce a resentment in those of us who live in the 'old country'. Indeed more, because added to our anger is the unbearable shame at what our detestable Government has done in destroying the most magnificent empire known to man. The names of those who for their own paltry ends contrived it are stained for all time.

Nevertheless, rage serves one useful purpose: it gives a keener edge to our determination that Great Britain shall be rescued from bondage to Cosmopolis and our overseas relationships as far as possible restored, perhaps made even stronger than before the debacle. I wrote at the beginning of the sadness which overwhelmed us as the new year took over from the old, but underneath that sorrow the cold steel of our resolve was further tempered, and our will to fight on made absolute.

In any war, whether military or political, it is useful to know not only who mans the enemy's front line, but the forces at the base and behind the base, who design the strategy and provide the munitions. We have no difficulty in recognising the front-liners—they are in our own country, men whose faces appear nauseatingly often in the newspapers and on the 'box'. But what of those more modest operators at the base concerned not with publicity but with power, who are they?

* * * *

Cabinet Minister Davies gave us the clue mentioned when in a candid moment he declared that the international corporation had more to offer mankind than had the nation state. This clearly indicated the projected end of nationhood. As the New Year took over, Great Britain was duly placed on the federal conveyor belt to her contemplated complete annihilation at the end of the decade. The political analysts know better than to ask what of the successor states, the international corporations.

Many multinational companies exist, some working in close association with British firms. In aerospace, for example, there is VEW, a German concern which has absorbed Fokkers in Holland, through which its tentacles embrace Avions Marcel Dassault-Brequet Aviation of France, a parity interest in the Belgian company Sabca and a complete monopoly in Holland. Actively participating are Messerschmitt-Bolkow-Blohm of Germany, Rolls-Royce Snecma of France, Fairey of Belgium and Hawker Siddeley of Britain. How many years will it be before the entire British aircraft industry passes into the maws of this gigantic outfit? Ten? Perhaps as few as five.

Several other supranational concerns could be used as the foundation-stones of future monopolies in E.E.C. industries—the tie-up between Agfa-Gevaert in chemicals, a Belgian German merger approved by the powerful Bayer AG combine; Pirelli-Dunlop in the tyre business; Estel, formed into a steel combine by Dutch and German interests.

Apart from multinational companies, there are huge industrial giants within each E.E.C. component, conglomerates covering pretty well the whole industrial, commercial and (above all) financial spectrum. Thus in Belgium there is the Societe Generale de Belgique which runs in double harness with the Societe de Banque and controls no less than seventy-two companies, which in their turn own nearly two hundred subsidiaries. Its range covers banking, non-ferrous metals, steel, cement, insurance, public works, engineering, textiles, paper, industrial diamonds, diamond tools, public utilities, mechanical and electrical manufacturing, shipping, fertilisers—the lot. Another giant Belgian company is the Compagnie Bruxelles Lambert, a Rothschild concern, which, after merging with three other holding companies, now looks after banking, insurance, real estate, breweries, food, oil, public utilities and steel and metal goods.

* * * *

In France the Societe des Usine Chimaques Rhone-Poulena could well become the bride of I.C.I., while the state owned Renault, with its immense power of patronage, direct and indirect, over private companies, has all that it takes to create a monolithic motor industry for the whole of Europe. Vast German concerns such as Thyssen, Krupp, Bayer, Volkswagenwerke, Siemens and I.B.M. are too well known to require description. The same applies to Holland's Philips, Royal Dutch and Unilever. Moreover, in the world of retail trade, every country within the E.E.C. has its own brands of Marks & Spencers, Woolworths and Great Universal Stores.

The British people (or those of them foolish enough to accept the Government's word) have been led to believe that one of the great advantages of entering Europe will be the spur to competition. Can anybody seriously suppose that all these titanic Continental complexes have eased Britain's progress into the Common Market for the sheer joy of friendly rivalry? Is it not certain that Britain is being drawn into the vortex not to give a keener edge to competition, but at the first, second or third remove to smash it by absorbing the competitors? For the same reason the vast British financial, industrial and commercial interests, using bodies such as the Royal Institute of International Affairs, Political and Economic Planning and the Confederation of British Industries as out-riders, have pressed the Government —not that it needed much pressing—to abandon national sovereignty and thereby facilitate their incorporation in massive monopolistic conglomerates extending from the Shannon to the Elbe.

The logic of this nefarious conspiracy is as clear as the facts are undeniable. Despite all the tenets of the Manchester School, financial and industrial capitalism has progressed at an accelerated rate ever further from the free play of the market towards rationalisation and, its twin brother, nationalisation. During the last several years, takeover bids have followed take-over bids, in every sphere of activity one merger has been succeeded by still larger mergers, not only in our own country, but throughout the world. As we know, in a large number of instances British companies have joined forces with Continental companies to form supranational mergers, but this is not enough for the new unhappy lords. To facilitate the working of the iniquitous banking system, to pave the road towards monopoly for the financial, industrial and commercial tycoons, to eliminate governmental interference and to reduce human beings to regimented groups of producers and consumers, it has been determined that mankind must come under the central control, politically, economically and strategically, of a single world authority.

* * * *

By far the most important step towards this end as yet taken is the incarceration of Great Britain inside the European prison-house devised by the hacks who drew up the Treaty of Rome. Independence, Finance Capitalism's greatest enemy, has to be destroyed. This requires that monopolies within the magic circle of patronage should have recourse to uniform trust laws wherewith to scotch would-be monopolists beyond the international financial pale. It no less strongly demands that national governments, now labouring under covert pressures, should become the overt instruments of the Money Power as a prelude to being phased out, or at any rate scaled down to provincial status, in favour of European Federation. Henceforward, declared Rothschild's Pompidou, there will no longer be European nations, only the European man.

That, however, is a grotesque over-simplification of the true intent. What has been designed is an all-embracing plutocracy, in which the holders of financial power are to have sole masterdom. Europe will be controlled through a system of giant combines with interlocking directorships, with holding companies within still larger holding companies, creating a maze of concealed interests all concerned with the exploitation of a continent of serfs.

Ivor Benson, the distinguished South African writer, has shown in his book *The Opinion Makers* how virtually impossible it is to track down the ownership of the English-speaking newspapers, even in his own numerically small country. The overall truth is of course known—the Rothschild-Oppenheimer Empire commands the field—but it cannot be known by the research-worker who is led through interminable holding companies which branch out in all directions and frequently double back on their tracks. Much more gigantic will be the European Leviathan operating over a huge area wherein monopolies, combines and conglomerates make common cause in a world-wide labyrinth, created by Banksterdom to conceal the dictatorship of High Finance.

* * * *

Whatever Pompidou may say about European man, the fact is that the financial, industrial and commercial complex which, outside most men's knowledge, regulates their lives, is not an emanation of the European brain. Historically, until the last three centuries Europe's economic life has been in the main the development of arts and crafts within an honest-to-goodness producer-consumer relationship based upon the open market. They were alien minds which invented the unholy modern system, with all its overt convolutions and subterranean intricacies aimed at the attainment of complete economic—and therefore political—power. Paterson the agent notwithstanding, they were alien minds which hit upon the most audacious and pernicious idea of commanding the key positions by issuing to the people the people's own credit as a debt repayable by the people to their financial overlords.

Thus we are led to the inescapable conclusion that the European Economic Community, like the Soviet Union, is an alien concept, and that Britain's adherence, involving as it does the spurning of overseas loyalties and a potential death-blow to Britain's own nationhood, is the result of alien pressures upon British tools anxious for personal advancement.

In following this train of thought let us consider, for the time being, just one aspect of our predicament. As from January 1, we have been ruled by a European Council of Ministers and a European Commission which are specifically required by the Treaty of Rome to owe allegiance to no national government. To whom, then, is allegiance owed if not to the peoples of Europe through their parliaments? Clearly to the largest international banking and industrial vested interests. It is therefore illuminating to learn that the British designated Director General for Industrial Affairs in the E.E.C. is Mr. Ronald Grierson, possessor of an impeccable British name. Grierson has been described as having "an unimpeachably European background", which is certainly no exaggeration. He is at present chairman of the Orion Bank, a multi-national financial group in the City of London, for which position his long association with the merchant bankers SG Warburg fully qualified him. Born in Nuremberg in 1921, he had a cosmopolitan education at the Pasteur Lycee, Highgate School and Balliol College, Oxford. He became Grierson by deed Poll in 1943, having been born with the somewhat less British-sounding name of Griessmann.

Only a pointer, admittedly, but a significant one. With Rothschild planning Governmental priorities at home and Warburg directing our entry into the Common Market, we have no excuse for failing to recognise our masters. Indeed, it should be all too obvious that the E.E.C. is one vast cattle-pen wherein the Gentiles are being herded for supervision, regimentation and exploitation.

* * * *

Stated in general, non-racial terms the forthright European mentality has been conquered by a mentality far more subtle. If that subtlety were a constant, the danger to Britain and Europe might be even more formidable than it is. Our hope lies in the fact, demonstrated several times in history, that the subtle operators when they see success ahead tend to overplay their hand. We believe that the messment which must follow the creation of the European Community will prove to be the most extravagant over-playing of any hand since time began.

Should this belief be correct, the day of the counter-revolution lies close ahead. The qualities required to take full advantage of it for the restoration of our nationhood and our overseas relationships are (in the absence of cunning) highly developed intelligence, dauntless courage and a willingness for personal sacrifice equal to anything needed in a shooting war. The call is not to die for our country and our kind, but to live for them with total selflessness—if anything, a more exacting demand.

Are Britons at home and in British lands overseas prepared to meet it? The answer will decide not only their future but whether or not they are to have a future they can call their own. To those who can read, the message has been spelled out, the enemy all but named. The important thing to remember is that to overcome the enemy we do not have to fight an alien breed. Our quarrel is with the political poltroons who, though puffed up with conceit of high office, would become woebegone and defeated creatures were the enemy's patronage withdrawn. The war to be fought is a political war but to succeed we must keep in mind that above all things that it is a civil war, waged against a massive array of British traitors.

* * * *

Pray Heaven that all Britons who abominate high treason will rally to the loyalist cause and, once embattled, stand firm in the grand tradition of their race. Those of us who, knowing what portends, stay aloof from the battle for the future will deservedly be written off as contemptible accessories after the fact of murder—the murder of a once superb nation and family of nations.

Appendix 1: The Treaty of Rome and Growth of the European Union

"The system of 'imperial preference' in British trade which had been declared in the 1932 Import Duties Act continued after the Second World War. In the 1950s Britain still enjoyed strong trading connections with the Commonwealth countries, but there was much feeling that the nation's trading relationships should be more fully developed in Europe.

Treaty of Rome 1957

In 1957 the Treaty of Rome established the European Economic Community which aimed to create a large European 'free trade area'. Initial British reluctance to seek membership of the Community was set aside by a decline in economic performance in the late 1950s, as compared with other European countries. In 1960 a British application to join the Community was rejected. A new application was made in 1967 and negotiations eventually began in October 1970.

The question of whether Britain should sign the Treaty of Accession was debated in the House of Commons in October 1971. Domestic opinion was strongly against membership and there was strong concern over whether the terms negotiated were good enough for Britain. Doubts over many issues affecting Britain's future were aired in a debate that lasted six days.

Britain Joins the European Economic Community

The Treaty was signed by Edward Heath, the British Prime Minister, in Brussels on 22 January 1972. The European Communities Bill was then introduced in the House of Commons to give parliamentary assent to Britain's membership of the EEC. Although the bill itself consisted of only 12 clauses (accepting all previous EEC regulations, the Treaty of Rome, and the terms of entry), it was subject to some 300 hours of debate before becoming law.

Britain's membership of what was then primarily an economic union came into effect on 1 January 1973. Since then the Community has developed into a much broader entity, the European Union, which was formally created by the Treaty of Maastricht of 1992. The terms of Britain's agreement to the Treaty received parliamentary approval in the European Communities (Amendment) Act of 1993, and the Union came into force in November 1993."

Source: http://www.parliament.uk/about/living-heritage/transformingsociety/tradeindustry/importexport/overview/europe/under the Open Parliament Licence v3.0

About A.K. Chesterton

Arthur Kenneth Chesterton was born at the Luipaards Vlei gold mine, Krugersdorp, South Africa where his father was an official in 1899.

In 1915 unhappy at school in England A.K. returned to South Africa. There and without the knowledge of his parents, and having exaggerated his age by four years, he enlisted in the 5th South African Infantry.

Before his 17th birthday he had been in the thick of three battles in German East Africa. Later in the war he transferred as a commissioned officer to the Royal Fusiliers and served for the rest of the war on the Western Front being awarded the Military Cross in 1918 for conspicuous gallantry.

Between the wars A.K. prospected for diamonds before becoming a journalist, first in South Africa and then in England. Alarmed at the economic chaos threatening Britain, he joined Sir Oswald Mosley in the B.U.F and became prominent in the movement. In 1938, he quarrelled with Mosley's policies and left the movement.

When the Second World War started he rejoined the army, volunteered for tropical service and went through all the hardships of the great push up from Kenya across the wilds of Jubaland through the desert of the Ogaden and into the remotest parts of Somalia. He was afterwards sent down the coast to join the Somaliland Camel Corps and intervene in the inter-tribal warfare among the Somalis.

In 1943 his health broke down and he was invalided out of the army with malaria and colitis, returning to journalism. In 1944, he became deputy editor and chief leader writer of *Truth*.

In the early 1950s A.K. established *Candour* and founded the League of Empire Loyalists which for some years made many colourful headlines in the press worldwide. He later took that organisation into The National Front, and served as its Chairman for a time.

A.K. Chesterton died in 1973.

A.K. Chesterton

About The A.K. Chesterton Trust

The A.K. Chesterton Trust was formed by Colin Todd and the late Miss. Rosine de Bounevialle in January 1996 to succeed and continue the work of the now defunct Candour Publishing Co.

The objects of the Trust are stated as follows:

"To promote and expound the principles of A.K. Chesterton which are defined as being to demonstrate the power of, and to combat the power of International Finance, and to promote the National Sovereignty of the British World."

Our aims include:

- *Maintaining and expanding the range of material relevant to A.K. Chesterton and his associates throughout his life.*

- *To preserve and keep in-print important works on British Nationalism in order to educate the current generation of our people.*

- *The maintenance and recovery of the sovereign independence of the British Peoples throughout the world.*

- *The strengthening of the spiritual and material bonds between the British Peoples throughout the world.*

- *The resurgence at home and abroad of the British spirit.*

We will raise funds by way of merchandising and donations.

We ask that our friends make provision for *The A.K. Chesterton Trust* in their will.

The A.K. Chesterton Trust has a **duty** to keep *Candour* in the ring and punching.

CANDOUR: To defend national sovereignty against the menace of international finance.

CANDOUR: To serve as a link between Britons all over the world in protest against the surrender of their world heritage.

Subscribe to Candour

CANDOUR SUBSCRIPTION RATES FOR 10 ISSUES.

U.K. £30.00
Europe 50 Euros.
Rest of the World £45.00.
USA $60.00.

All Airmail. Cheques and Postal Orders, £'s Sterling only, made payable to *The A.K. Chesterton Trust*. (Others, please send cash by **secure post**, $ bills or Euro notes.)

Payment by Paypal is available. Please see our website **www.candour.org.uk** for more information.

Candour Back Issues

Back issues are available. 1953 to the present.

Please request our back issue catalogue by sending your name and address with two 1st class stamps to:

The A.K. Chesterton Trust, BM Candour, London, WC1N 3XX, United Kingdom.

Alternatively, see our website at **www.candour.org.uk** where you can order a growing selection on-line.

British Peoples League

Britons Unite Worldwide

Box 691, Minden, Ontario. K0M 2K0, Canada.
www.britishpeoplesleague.com

Broadsword

The official supporting publication of the British Movement

For a sample copy of their 24-page Journal send £2.00 payable to *Broadsword* at:
PO Box 6, Heckmondwicke, WF16 0XF, England

Heritage and Destiny

Nationalist News & Views

For a sample copy of Heritage & Destiny, please send £5.00 payable to the same at:
40 Birkett Drive, Preston, PR2 6HE, England

The London Forum

The London Forum hosts regular meetings in Central London on a Pan-Nationalist theme with a wide range of speakers from across Europe and the World.

For more information please email: jezenglish@yahoo.co.uk

The A.K. Chesterton Trust **Reprint Series**

1. Creed of a Fascist Revolutionary & Why I Left Mosley - A.K. Chesterton.

2. The Menace of World Government & Britain's Graveyard - A.K. Chesterton.

3. What You Should Know About The United Nations - The League of Empire Loyalists.

4. The Menace of the Money-Power - A.K. Chesterton.

5. The Case for Economic Nationalism - John Tyndall.

6. Sound the Alarm! - A.K. Chesterton.

7. Six Principles of British Nationalism - John Tyndall.

8. B.B.C. - A National Menace - A.K. Chesterton.

9. Stand by the Empire - A.K. Chesterton.

10. Tomorrow. A Plan for the British Future - A.K. Chesterton.

11. The British Constitution and the Corruption of Parliament - Ben Greene.

12. Very High Finance & The Policy of a Patriot - Cahill & Strasser

Other Titles from *The A.K. Chesterton Trust*

Leopard Valley – by A.K. Chesterton.

Juma The Great – by A.K. Chesterton.

The New Unhappy Lords – by A.K. Chesterton.

Facing The Abyss – by A.K. Chesterton.

The History of the League of Empire Loyalists – by H. McNeile & R. Black

The A.B.C. of Politics - by Rosine de Bouneviale

Hidden Government- by John Creagh Scott

All the above titles are available from The A.K. Chesterton Trust, BM Candour, London, WC1N 3XX, UK. (www.candour.org.uk)

Printed in Great Britain
by Amazon